John Adair is currently visiting Professor in Leadership Studies at the University of Exeter and an international consultant to a wide variety of organizations in business, government, the voluntary sector, education and health. He has been named as one of the forty people worldwide who have contributed most to the development of management thought and practice.

Educated at St Paul's School, John Adair has enjoyed a varied and colourful career. He has served in the Arab Legion, worked as a deckhand on an Arctic trawler and had a spell as an orderly in a hospital operating theatre. After Cambridge he became senior lecturer in Military History and Leadership Training Adviser at the Royal Military Academy, Sandhurst before becoming Director of Studies at St George's House in Windsor Castle and then Assistant Director of the Industrial Society. He writes extensively on both management and history.

John Adair is married with three children. He lives near Guildford in Surrey.

Other titles in John Adair's
Effective Management series:

EFFECTIVE *Leadership*

EFFECTIVE *Decision making*

EFFECTIVE *Time Management*

EFFECTIVE *Teambuilding*

EFFECTIVE *Innovation*

All are available from Pan Books,
priced £6.99.

JOHN ADAIR

EFFECTIVE
Motivation

How to get extraordinary results from everyone

PAN BOOKS

First published 1996 by Pan Books

an imprint of Macmillan General Books
25 Eccleston Place London SW1W 9NF
and Basingstoke

Associated companies throughout the world

ISBN 0 333 34476 5

1 3 5 7 9 8 6 4 2

A CIP catalogue record for this book is available from
the British Library

Typeset by CentraCet Limited, Cambridge
Printed and bound in Great Britain by
Mackays of Chatham plc, Chatham, Kent

'There is not a single person who has not had great moments, has not risen to rare occasions.'
Ernest Dimnet

'Give me fire and I will give you light.'
Arab proverb

To my son, James Adair

CONTENTS

4   NOT FOR BREAD ALONE

5   THE HYGIENE FACTORS

6   THE MOTIVATORS

PART TWO: BRIDGING THE GAP

7   THE THREE-CIRCLES MODEL

8   BALANCING THE BALLOONS

9   LEADERSHIP AND MOTIVATION

10   INSPIRING OTHERS

11   THE FIFTY-FIFTY PRINCIPLE

PART THREE: HOW TO DRAW OUT THE BEST FROM PEOPLE

12   BE MOTIVATED YOURSELF

13   SELECT PEOPLE WHO ARE ALREADY MOTIVATED

14   SET CHALLENGING BUT REALISTIC TARGETS

15 REMEMBER THAT PROGRESS MOTIVATES

16 TREAT EACH PERSON AS AN INDIVIDUAL

17 PROVIDE FAIR REWARDS

18 GIVE RECOGNITION

INTRODUCTION

Not long ago I met a friend in Thorpe's bookshop in Guildford.

'Hello, John, what are you doing these days?' she said.

'Quite a few things,' I replied, 'among them writing a book on motivation.'

'Haven't you covered that ground fairly thoroughly in your other books? Why another? Surely your model of the three-circles is not out of date?'

'No, it isn't, but the world is changing . . .'

'Yes,' my friend interrupted, 'it certainly is and leadership seems to be coming to the fore, but not the old style of individual leadership. Perhaps we are all leaders now.'

Later I reflected upon the paradox she had presented to me. 'Take away paradox from the thinker and you have the professor,' said Kierkegaard. A transformation of managers into leaders . . . yet everyone at work is a leader and a manager. People whose job it is to motivate others . . . yet only people who are self-motivated will find work and stay in employment today.

You wrestle with such paradoxes; you don't resolve them. This book is the fruit of my own wrestling. Its primary purpose, however, is to encourage you as a manager to think through these issues in some depth in order to improve your powers of leadership in a complex and demanding environment. In places it may not be an easy book to read, but I hope you will find it a rewarding one. It may serve to underpin your own philosophy of management, or it may trigger off questions and ideas that lead you to reformulate your own perspective – at least on this vital issue of motivation.

THE BOOK'S AIMS

Under this broad umbrella of purpose I see the book as having three more specific aims, all designed to help you to build effectively and to work with the grain of human nature not against it. Its focus is the people who work with, for, or under you. But the principles apply much more widely. Some of them will be directly relevant to your relations with suppliers and customers. Others will apply in voluntary and social activities, or even in the home. Ever tried motivating teenage children?

How can you improve your ability to inspire or motivate other people?

1. *You need to UNDERSTAND what motivates you and others at work*. You'll notice that I put *you* first. The reason for doing so is that we use ourselves as analogies for understanding others. 'No person really knows about other human beings,' said the novelist John Steinbeck. 'The best he or she can do is to suppose that they are like themselves.' If you have an accurate picture of what motivates you, you will be in a far better position to understand what motivates others.
2. *You need an AWARENESS of both the general and the individual dimensions of motivation*. Let me explain

briefly what I mean. In this book you can learn plenty of
generalizations about people, including 'individuals'.
These are useful. But they are only half the story. Think of
yourself – how complex and unique you are. To motivate
anyone beyond the 'stick-and-carrot' level means you have
to know him or her as an individual person by name.

3. *You need to develop your SKILLS as a leader of others*.
As a manager you are called now to be a leader, and
leadership includes the ability to motivate and inspire
others. How do you do it? What you are and what you
know matters, but what you *do* as a leader in those three-
circles of team or organizational need – task, team and
individual – is vital. For high motivation, like happiness,
is largely a by-product. Hence the considerable overlap
between leadership and motivation.

THE BOOK'S PLAN

The book's plan stems logically from these three aims or
areas of purpose. It is divided into three parts, though their
subject matter overlaps considerably.

- Part One focuses on those theories and research into human
  motivation at work that are now a recognized part of
  classical managerial thought. Therefore some of them, at least
  in outline, may be familiar to you already. My contribution is
  two-fold. First, I have tried to make them more intelligible.
  Secondly, in the conclusion at the end of each section I have
  drawn out the *practical implications* for managers.

- Part Two bridges the gap – some may see it as a chasm –
  between the general philosophy of human nature that

underpins so much of the theory in Part One with the more focused strategies for creating a highly motivated team in Part Three. First, using the integrating powers of the three-circle model, the contents of Part One are pulled into a shape you can use. Then your role as a leader in management is fully explored.

- Part Three contains seven practical strategies – the main channels of effective motivation. Together they should answer your question: *How can I draw out the best from others?* The principles, of course, apply to your organization as well as to you. But I have written them in such a way that you can act on them without waiting for your organization to change. For here, as nowhere else, if you are not part of the solution you are part of the problem.

HOW TO USE THIS BOOK

Please don't feel that you have to start at the beginning and read through to the end! You may, for example, wish to look first at the practical strategies in Part Three, and then trace their roots or pedigree back to Part One. Alternatively, you may prefer to move from the more general principles and concepts to the particular and practical steps recommended in the second part. Choose the approach that suits you best.

You may have already glanced through the book. If so, you will have noticed that in Part Two each chapter is accompanied by a Checklist. The questions in these checklists are designed mainly to help you apply what you know or what you learn to your own situation. You may find it useful to complete the checklists after a second reading of the book. They also serve as refreshers if you later decide – as I hope you will – to conduct a personal self-review of progress after three months.

Another line of approach is first to complete the checklists toward the end of each chapter in Part Three. Then focus your attention on those areas where you are scoring on the low side.

In order not to hold you up unnecessarily on your first fast-track read I have enclosed some material – relevant research and other contributions – in Boxes within the text. Again, be selective about them. You can skip them without any loss to the main themes of the book if you prefer.

The CONCLUSIONS (Key Points) at the end of each chapter in Part Three are designed to give you an *aide-mémoire* of the whole contents. Just for fun I have slipped in occasionally one or two extra points – ones you won't find in the preceding chapter.

In summary: the core purpose of the following pages is to stimulate your own thought and ideas on this most interesting of subjects. They should lead you to see some practical ways in which you can better motivate yourself and others.

The test of wanting is doing.

PART ONE

UNDERSTANDING MOTIVATION

Understanding is usually the necessary prelude to intelligent and effective action in any field. When it comes after action rather than before it we call it experience. It is especially important where people are concerned. Theories and research on motivation will not give you any sure and certain answers. But the true function of such ideas is to stimulate your own thought. I have selected only those theories or findings that have the proven power to do just that.

By the time you have read the chapters and summaries in Part One you should have:

1. revised your knowledge of the main THEORIES and RESEARCH concerning people at work which emanated from the United States of America in the mid twentieth century.
2. put them in the context of some broader PRINCIPLES that govern human nature in all situations where exchange is involved.
3. identified the main PRACTICAL IMPLICATIONS for managing people today which are suggested by the theories and researches.

1

WHAT IS MOTIVATION?

Why do you do anything? Why do you feel drawn to some forms of work and repelled by others? Perhaps the first step to answering these difficult questions is to explore the central concept of motivation.

Long words like motivation, innovation and communication usually have Latin origins. Motivation comes from motive, which in turn derives from the Latin verb *movere*, to move. So a motive, quite simply, is something that *moves you to action*.

Characteristically these words motive or motivation, however, suggest that something *within you* is at work, impelling or driving you forwards. It may be a need, desire or emotion, but it leads you to act – and to act in a certain way.

Notice that these inner impulses, however strong, are not going to be effective unless they engage your will and get you going or moving. To will is to decide. It's the action of deciding to do something; it implies a conscious intention towards initiating a chosen action. Your motivation will be evident in your behaviour. You will show definite signs of having a deliberate or fixed desire or intention.

The difference between having motives and being motivated to act is illustrated in the following story. See if you can identify the probable murderer.

THE CASE OF THE MURDERED TYCOON

Edwin Gettings, one of the richest men in the world, fell over the side of his luxury yacht *Serena* in the Bay of Naples in the early hours of the morning, not long after a drunken party on the afterdeck had ended with the guests lurching to their cabins. At first it appeared to be an accident until the Italian coroner discovered traces of arsenic in his blood, and declared it a case of murder.

There were three suspects on board that night, each with a motive to kill. Damon Gettings hated his father for refusing to pay his gambling debts. Sharon, the tycoon's secretary, had been having an affair with him and she felt outraged and incensed when he refused that night to divorce his fourth wife and marry her. Getting's valet, Robert, stood to inherit one million dollars in his master's will, but he had been threatened with dismissal that night for refusing the homosexual advances of one of Gettings' major Chinese customers. An open container of arsenic was in the yacht's storeroom because several disease-ridden rats had been spotted on board. Who killed Edwin Gettings?

(Turn to page 13.)

The signs of motivation – such as energy and determination – are what prospective employers are probably looking for when selecting job candidates. Later they will seek to develop or deepen these characteristics. One important survey of major European business organizations listed all the words that are used in their paperwork related to selection, training and appraisal. The terms relating to motivation are given in the table below. They provide a useful guide to the terms that managers use today.

ASSOCIATED TERMS	ASSOCIATED QUALITIES
Approach to work	Energy
Orientation to work	Drive
Application	Tenacity
Willingness	Determination
Dedication	Strength of purpose
Alignment of person and organization	Purposeful
Commitment	
Work appetite	

Figure 1.1   *Some Synonyms for Motivation* (From *What Makes a Manager?* A Report by the Institute of Manpower Studies, 1988.)

Your 'will' acts as a complex signal box at the junctions between your needs or desires and your possible actions. It signifies the facility we all have for initiating conscious or intentional action. It's integral to the concept of being a person. Because the exercise of our wills implies the use of conscious reason it separates us from animals on the one hand, and computers and machines on the other.

For centuries philosophers have discussed the extent of 'free will', as they call it. Are we free to choose or decide? How much conscious control do we exercise over our actions? Are we programmed to respond to stimuli? Do we resemble computers? It's an endless debate. Common sense, however, does tell us that for practical purposes we do have free will. We can move the levers of action in the signal box of our wills. By decision making we give the green light to some trains of action; others we stop dead in their tracks by switching on the red light.

This capacity to edit your instincts or impulses – acting on some and ignoring others – used to be called *will-power*. That phrase itself now sounds rather dated. It was also employed to describe the force or energy that people display in executing their will or intention.

THE SONG OF THE SIRENS

The part the will plays in inhibiting action is well illustrated by the story of Odysseus and the Sirens, sea-songstresses who lived on an island near Scylla and Charybdis. Sailors enticed by the Sirens' magical song land on the island and perish; the meadow is full of decaying corpses. But Odysseus, in order he would hear this ravishing sound, had himself lashed to the mast as the ship approached the island. His sailors, their ears stopped with plugs, ignored his cries to release him as he was filled with insane desire. The ropes of will-power held him fast.

When Jason and the Argonauts sailed past the island of the Sirens they were accompanied by the famous Thracian singer and lyre-player, Orpheus. Orpheus, who it was said could charm trees, wild beasts and even stones with his music, began to sing. So enchanting was the sound that Jason and his crew completely ignored the Siren voices. They rowed past the island to safety. Our word *incentive* comes from the Latin word 'to sing'.

A motive, then, is an inner need or desire – conscious, or semi-conscious or perhaps unconscious – which operates on your will and leads to action of one kind or another. Of course you may have motives that do not issue in any action. They don't get past the signal box. You may, on the other hand, do things that are apparently motiveless. Here there is a motive but it may be so opaque or unconscious that neither you nor anyone else can describe it. Or there may be runaway trains, ones that rush blindly past all the warning lights.

Such runaway trains are often powered mainly by *emotion*. Like motive, our word *emotion* also comes from that same Latin verb 'to move'. But it's worth noting how often we experience emotions that are unrelated to action. A tragedy, for example, seen on television may move you to tears, but you probably won't do anything about it. Of course, sometimes deeply felt emotion may become a motive for practical change.

WHO KILLED EDWARD GETTINGS?

Damon, Sharon and Robert all had motives for killing Edwin Gettings, but moral scruples or practical considerations deterred them all from being motivated to act and carry out the killing. In fact Gettings, aware that his financial empire was about to crumble, killed himself by lacing his last whiskey and soda with arsenic and then jumping overboard.

ON MIXED MOTIVES

Any single action can be driven forwards by more than one motive. In other words, our motives are often mixed.

When Sarah's husband died after a long illness leaving her with an overdraft at the bank and three children to bring up alone she was sure that she would never marry again, for she loved him very deeply. But several years later at a dinner party she met James, a widower with two young children of his own. Eventually they decided to get married. 'To be honest I am not in love with him,' Sarah told her best friend, 'but he is kind and has a sense of humour and he really cares for me. I enjoy his company, and I have been feeling very lonely recently. I need someone to look after me! Moreover, he can be a father to my three boys – perhaps they need a man in their lives. Also he can give me some companionship and security when I am older and the children have left home.'

In the course of time Sarah's love for James did grow, but that is another story. As this discussion with her friend reveals she was honest about her primary motives: the needs for companionship and emotional security. She had a number of lesser motives which added up to one larger motivation: one strong enough for her to accept James' offer of marriage.

Most of us most of the time do act from mixed motives. As we shall see in the next chapter, this factor makes some of our calculations and decisions extremely complex. Notice here, however, that mixed motives are not necessarily weaker, more impure or lacking in integrity. A composite bow, made from different materials, will shoot arrows further than a conventional bow made from the best wood available.

MOTIVES AT DIFFERENT LEVELS OF CONSCIOUSNESS

Like Sarah in the story above, we often feel the need to give a *reason* or *reasons* for why we do things. If you ever have the misfortune to end up standing in the dock in a court of law you will be required to do so! Reasons and motives are often used as virtual synonyms to describe what stimulates one to action. But reason more specifically implies a logical or rational justification, either to oneself or to others, for an action. This may be done – by citing relevant facts and circumstances – so that the action becomes understandable.

This process of giving a natural explanation can tip over into what is called *rationalization*, which means to attribute one's actions to rational and creditable motives without analysis of true (especially unconscious) motives. The first difficulty, of course, is that we do not always know what our motives are. We may be able to feel them, but we cannot label them. Secondly, we all like to appear in a favourable light to ourselves if not to others. We feel – rightly or wrongly – that if we were honest about our motives, it would cause negative or hostile reactions. Very possibly we should go down in their estimate. Therefore sometimes we offer plausible but untrue reasons for our conduct, with the implicit or explicit intention of misleading others.

It follows that it's not always easy to detect rationalization in ourselves or others. How do you discern the truth in a web of reasons which may have been spun in order to justify what has been done – or not done?

So rationalizations may be put up quite deliberately like smokescreens to hide your real motives – ones which for one reason or another you don't want known. Perhaps you feel they may discredit you. Or they may be more like mists arising from a swamp in so far as we are attempting to give reasons for actions that are vague even to ourselves. For their springs lie hidden in the marshes of the unconscious.

Of course consciousness and unconsciousness are not black-and-white states. They are more like two end-areas of a spectrum, with many different station stops on the line between them. Indeed one real difficulty in thinking clearly about motivation as a subject is that so much of it is naturally unconscious.

THE STICK-AND-CARROT THEORY

To *MOTIVATE* goes beyond *MOTIVE* because it is some-thing that you can do to another person. Here to motivate means essentially that you provide *a person with a motive or incentive to do* something or other. By so doing you are *initiating* their action or behaviour. To put it another way, you are *stimulating* the interest of that person to activity.

The oldest theory on earth – and still the most wide-spread – is known by the proverbial phrases 'stick-and-carrot' and 'carrot-and-stick'. You may think it odd that I dignify it by using the word *theory*. After all, there are no academic books or dissertations on it. None the less, it is a theory. And it does rest on certain assumptions.

Just to show you how deep-rooted the theory is, our word *stimulus* comes from the Latin noun for a *goad*, the steel-tipped stick used to prod animals and keep them going against their will or desire.

Imagine that you have an immobile donkey. One way to get it to move in the direction you require is by beating it with a stick or prodding it with a goad. The other way is to hold a carrot in front of its nose. From your angle it doesn't matter too much which method works, just as long as the donkey moves forward without you having to use up your precious energy by forcing or dragging it every protesting step. After all, the donkey you own is supposed to save you energy, not consume it.

With either the carrot or stick you are helping the donkey to make up its mind. The carrot as a form of fast food meets its hunger need. It will obviously be more effective as a stimulus to movement if you ensure that the donkey is hungry. If he isn't hungry or if he has eaten too many carrots, then your proferred carrot will probably not work. If you beat the donkey it may well make up its mind to move in order to stop the pain by getting out of your range. Underlying this movement will be the strong dislike and fear of pain common to all animals, including ourselves.

Again you may be able to make this goad or stimulus more effective by simply showing the big stick. The donkey's fear of the stick, stored in his memory by the cause-effect experience of past beatings, will do the rest. You can also choose a donkey with a low pain threshold and a high degree of anxiety.

Let me say at once that I am not advocating the maltreatment of animals! But the proverbial saying about sticks and carrots does illustrate the deepest held if often semi-conscious, theory or assumption about motivating others, namely that it essentially consists of providing rewards or punishments. For we tend to apply the same assumption to other people as we do to the proverbial donkey. Of course people are different. For one thing we can talk, and so we can know much more about what is going on in each other's minds. Also, humans are actively interested in attaining more goods than food and in avoiding more evils than those symbolized by the big stick.

The two great movers of the human mind are the desire of good, and the fear of evil.

Samuel Johnson

Both the carrot and the stick fall into a common category: they are both external stimuli. From being the goad used to urge on an animal, stimulus was extended to mean anything that provokes, increases or quickens bodily activity, and finally to include all that arouses, animates or gives more energy to the mind or spirit. Thus, apart from moving you to action, a stimulus could also arouse your interest or be something that satisfies or invigorates you. When you motivate others you are applying, consciously or unconsciously, a stimulus of one kind or another to their minds, hearts or spirits. It may be a positive one, such as offering a reward or inducement as an incentive. It may be a negative one, such as the threat of dire consequences if a change of position doesn't occur. Or it may be some combination of the two.

There is an analogy between humans and donkeys or teams of draught animals, otherwise the 'stick-and-carrot' theory wouldn't have persisted so long. But, like all analogies, it breaks down at a certain point. For individuals are qualitatively different from donkeys, hunting dogs, or horses. There is a third way of motivating people, which is by infusing them with your own spirit – through word and example.

CONCLUSION

Motivation is the sum of all that moves a person to action. Motives can be mixed. They can range from consensus to unconscious. Motives are necessary for action but not sufficient in themselves. For action to happen a decision has to be made or the will engaged. Hence the legal maxim: 'We must judge a person's motives from their overt actions.' The reasons we give for our actions, however, do not always correspond with our motives.

Motivation also extends to moving *others* to action. The traditional 'stick-and-carrot' theory suggests two 'motives' that we can apply – a reward or incentive on one hand and fear of the consequences on the other. These are external stimuli which draught animals are said to understand. But the 'stick-and-carrot' theory is only as good as the analogy on which it rests. You can move others in varying degrees, depending on the situation, by rewards or punishment. But human nature, especially our extraordinary powers of communication, opens a third way. You can stir up or stimulate a whole range of motives in others which have little to do with avoiding pain or seeking material rewards.

2

WHAT DO YOU EXPECT?

The 'carrot-and-stick' theory we have just explored is the common relative of the more rarefied 'expectancy theory' that you will find in the management textbooks.

Expectancy theory centres upon the conscious or rational process by which you calculate what you will get as opposed to what you will have to give. In animals it is an instinctive judgment.

A large soft-padded Canadian lynx chasing a snow rabbit through thick snow will only do so for about 200 metres. It then gives up. The food gained if it catches the rabbit will not replace the energy lost in the pursuit. It will chase a deer longer before making the same instinctive choice.

This approach doesn't contradict the needs-theory of Maslow and others, whose work will be discussed in more detail later. Nor is it an alternative. It merely focuses our attention at the crucial junction between motives (as needs, drives or desires) and action. It tries to take us into the signal box of the will and show what kind of computing takes place there. Expectancy theory has even attempted to reduce such judgements into formulae or equations.

ORIGINS OF EXPECTANCY THEORY

Motivational theories are sometimes put into two opposing camps, each supported by different philosophical assumptions about human nature. The behaviourists consider human behaviour to be reflexive and instinctive, governed by 'stimulus-response'; cognitive psychologists assume that individuals are basically rational and purposive, choosing goals and capable of modifying or altering their behaviour. Like most dichotomies it is ultimately a false one: one paradox of human nature is that we encompass both motivations, for they are no more than the ends of our particular spectrum. But the distinction is still useful.

Expectancy theory is clearly in the cognitive camp. An American psychologist named Edward C. Tolman is credited with formulating it first in the 1930s. He did so as a rejoinder to the prevailing behaviouralist philosophy of psychology at that time. Tolman suggested that human behaviour will be motivated by the conscious *expectations* more than response to stimulii. The expectations will be that the action in prospect will lead to a desired goal or outcome – hence the name 'expectancy theory'.

Supposing, for example, an individual worker needs a lot more money, perhaps to support a sick child. And supposing that he is assured that if he works harder he will receive more. Then it can be *predicted* – on expectancy-theory grounds – that the individual concerned will put in the necessary time and effort to win the desired reward. But if, on the other hand, such above-average industry only wins some words of praise then the individual concerned will rapidly tend to lose all interest. Individuals therefore are consciously self-interested. They behave in ways that are *instrumental* in achieving their valued outcomes.

Expectancy theory can be used to explain in part another phenomenon. In the Hawthorne experiments Elton Mayo had recorded that individual workers seem to adjust their own motivational levels to those of the group. See if you can apply the theory to interpreting the findings described in the next box.

THE HAWTHORNE STUDIES

The work of Elton Mayo at the Hawthorne works of Western Electric in the USA in the 1930s challenged some of the assumptions of scientific management, with its emphasis on the carrot-and-stick, and ushered in the 'human relations' movement. The studies emphasized the importance of social factors at work and the influence of informal group norms on satisfaction and productivity. Studies were designed to investigate the effect of various degrees of illumination, of rest pauses, and the length of the working day on the efficiency of workers assembling electrical components. No simple relationship was discovered. Rather, in some conditions – such as the investigation of illumination level – productivity rose regardless of experimental changes, while other studies showed apparently haphazard changes in output with no obvious explanation. Follow-up experiments and interviews with the workers showed that informal social groups within the organization influenced individual attitudes and job performance. One aspect of the Hawthorne studies, for example, provided an early account of output restriction. Men in the Bank Wiring Observation Room were paid on a system of group piecework for the whole department which meant that each man's earnings were affected by the output of every other man in the department. Yet the observers noted that fast workers in the group were restricting their output to hold their production within the informal group standard.

The Hawthorne researchers have been subjected to many criticisms. One critic, for example, argues that it was impossible to draw firm conclusions from the studies because of uncontrolled factors in the experimental design, and that the conclusions the experimenters drew from the findings neither follow from nor are supportable from their data. Yet the studies have been very influential. They led to the demise of economic man, motivated by monetary self-interest. Workers were shown not to be passive individuals responding to incentives or avoiding hard work as Taylor [the father of scientific management] had suggested but were *groups* of workers establishing informal group norms for production. The men seemed to establish their identity in the group and were more responsive to the social pressures of their group than to the control of management. But while the Hawthorne work was an advance on the scientific management view, it too is certainly not a complete view. Many individuals seem to care nothing for the group standard or the ostracism of their colleagues. These 'rate-busters' defy group standards and produce far more than average.

from D. R. Davies and V. J. Shackleton, *Psychology of Work* (1975)

If an individual worker values the esteem of others and his or her acceptance by the group and knows that exceptional output on a unilateral basis will anger these colleagues and disrupt the group, then you can predict that such an individual will conform – perfectly rationally – to the group norm of production.

MAKING IT MORE COMPLICATED

In 1964 an American psychologist, Victor H. Vroom, developed a rather more complicated formulation of an expectancy theory of work motivation. His theory appears to offer a way of measuring human motivation. The preference that the individual has for a particular outcome he called its *valence*. As a person may seek or avoid certain outcomes, or be ambivalent about them, valence can be *positive, negative* or *neutral*.

Vroom's term *subjective probability* describes the individual's expectation that behaviour would lead to a particular outcome. It's subjective because people will differ in their judgements of the relationships between their behaviour and outcomes. It may vary between 0 and 1, from no probability at all on one end to absolute certainty at the other. The strength of motivation to a particular action thus depends on both the *valence* of the outcome and the *subjective probability* of achieving it.

Vroom suggests that the 'force' of the individual's motivation to act in a particular way is

$$F = E \times V$$

where F = motivation to behave
E = the expectation (the subjective probability) that the behaviour will be followed by a particular outcome
V = the valence of the outcome
This is called the *expectancy equation*.

In most situations, however, several different outcomes will issue from a particular behaviour. The expectancy equation therefore has to be calculated across all these outcomes. The resultant equation is therefore:

$$F = \Sigma \ (E \times V)$$

The sign Σ is the Greek letter sigma, which here means 'add up all the values of the calculation in the brackets'.

Expectancy and valence are multiplied because when either E or V is zero, motivation is also going to be zero. This is what would be expected. If expectancy is added to valence, an unrealistic result is produced. If you believe that a given behaviour will certainly lead to a given result but place no value on that outcome, then you will not be motivated to go that way. But if you place a high value on an outcome while expecting that the probability of attaining it is zero, your motivation will again be zero. Only when both of the terms are positive can motivation be said to exist.

You can see that expectancy theory can be complex. Do you have to make this kind of calculation before you do anything? Are we really capable of doing this sort of analysis at conscious level? Possibly not, but our minds at a deeper than conscious level are capable of making complicated judgements of this nature.

One important contribution of expectancy theory is to remind us that, individual perceptions being different, the motivation and behaviour of individuals will vary considerably. Someone in the same circumstances as you may place a different valuation on the outcomes and respond quite differently. Notice the prominent role that your values play in the expectancy model of motivation.

James Kingfisher had worked for Bruno Merchant Bank for nine years when it became part of a much larger banking group. The new owners cut staff and increased performance targets for those who were left. They also wanted other changes.

'James,' said Martin Kay, the head of his section, one morning, 'I have some good news. We are being joined in Mergers and Acquisitions by Tom Forristall, who is one of the best in the business. You'll be able to learn a hell of a lot from him. But it means that we are all going to have to work much later in the evening – Tom's one of these workaholics but he really is bloody good. Of course our bonuses should all double.'

James went away and thought about it. Next morning he saw Martin in the corridor and told him he had decided to leave. 'I value my time in the evening with my children,' he said. 'I don't really need the extra money.'

'But don't you want to be a world-class deal-maker?' asked Martin. 'What an opportunity to pass by – it will never come again.'

'Nor will my children,' replied James with a smile.

We are bound to perceive people and situations differently because our values are as distinctive as our fingerprints. Values work the lights in the signal box of your will, saying yes to one train of action and no to another.

ON CALCULATION

The bare bones of the basic model are set out below. In this form the model is most understandable if it is regarded as the way a person deals with *individual* decisions, to do or not to do something, to go or not go, to apportion or not to apportion their time, energy and talents. This approach is based on the idea that people are self-activating organisms, and to some degree, control their own destiny and responses to pressures, that they can select their own goals and choose the paths towards them. Some versions of this approach have in fact been given the name of path-goal theories.

needs

'E' factors _____ the motivation calculus

results

The model in this form merely states that each individual has a set of *needs* and of *desired results.* That they decide how much 'E' (which stands for effort, energy, excitement, expenditure, etc.) to invest by doing a calculation. The process of calculation is not often as cold-blooded or deliberate as this description would suggest . . .

Charles Handy, *Understanding Organizations* (1993)

The difficulty with these various forms of the expectancy theory is that they presuppose a being called 'rational man'. We do, of course, all have reason – the intellectual power or faculty which we ordinarily employ in adapting thought or action to some end. But there are other elements in our nature which also influence the motivational calculus. Selfishness can bias us towards seeking to get more than we give. As an old German proverb says, 'A man has one eye on what he gives, but seven eyes on what he receives.' But generosity of spirit can also induce us to give more on occasions than we expect to receive.

CONCLUSION

Expectancy theory rests upon our natural or instinctive tendency to balance the value of expected benefits against the expenditure of energy. A rational calculation of the probabilities of the course of action securing the valued outcomes is involved. We can improve expectancy theory by extending it to encompass the more unconscious judgements of the mind. But it is only as good as the assumption on which it rests, namely that humans act rationally. It is this concept of rationality which needs further exploration. Most of us for most of the time are reasonable beings, which is why the 'stick-and-carrot' and the expectancy theories broadly work. But there are occasions when – perhaps irrationally – we want more than we are prepared to give – or give more than we expect to receive.

There is a law of equivalence in the reciprocal dealings, exchanges or transactions of the human spirit. If you give generously you will tend to receive in like measure. For example, if you pay those working for you above the market rates, then you have created one necessary condition for a matching 'above average' response from your partners. For a second example, if you give customers more than they bargained for, then they will tend to give you more of their business.

From the practical manager's viewpoint, there are two further lessons. Expectancy theory teaches you to ensure that the routes to desired outcomes for teams or individuals are as clear and as unequivocal as possible. Above all, it tells you that any two individuals in the same situation may *perceive* the rewards/punishments available in very different ways, according to their particular values or assessments of probabilities. Consquently we find that there are no universal panaceas for motivating others. Treat each person as an individual.

3

MASLOW'S HIERARCHY OF NEEDS

Perhaps no theory of motivation has been so influential on the thinking of managers as Abraham Maslow's hierarchy of needs. In essence, it suggests that a person is motivated not by external motives such as rewards or punishment but by an inner programme of *needs*. These needs are arranged in sets. When one set is satisfied, another comes into play. A satisfied need ceases to motivate.

Most probably you have read this theory before. Or you may have just heard about it. In this context it is worth exploring in some depth.

Can human needs be mapped? Are they related to each other? Does the satisfaction of one set of conscious needs trigger off into consciousness another set of previously unconscious needs? Abraham Maslow offers a confident answer to these questions:

'Man is a wanting animal and rarely reaches a state of complete satisfaction except for a short time. As one desire is satisfied, another pops up to take its place. When this is satisfied, still another comes into the foreground. It is characteristic of the human being throughout his whole life that he is practically always desiring something. We are faced then with the necessity of studying the relationships of all the motivations to each other and we are concomitantly faced with the necessity of giving up the motivational units in isolation if we are to achieve the broad understanding that we seek for.'

So declared Maslow in an article which first appeared in America in 1943. 'A Theory of Motivation', as it was entitled, was later republished in his book *Motivation and Personality* (1954), and has since become universally known.

In this seminal paper Maslow sought to establish 'some sort of hierarchy of prepotency' in the realm of basic human needs, and to comment upon the difference this hierarchy would make to our understanding of motivation. He identified five sets of need, which he saw as being in a dynamic relationship or hierarchy. If a person has an endless supply of bread, at once other needs emerge and they supersede the physiological needs in dominating the organism. And when these in turn are satisfied, yet higher needs emerge, and so on. This is what Maslow meant by asserting that the basic human needs are organized into a hierarchy of relative prepotency.

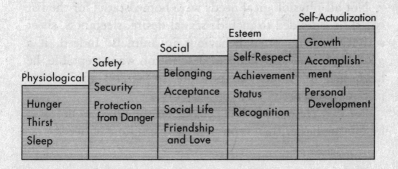

Figure 3.1 Maslow's Hierarchy of Needs

Although there isn't any evidence that he himself used the diagram, Maslow's theory of a hierarchy of prepotent needs is often set out in a triangle or pyramid model. But this has the disadvantage of showing the higher needs as smaller in size, whereas the reverse is true. Our capacity for food is limited, but our capacity for personal growth is by comparison limitless. Perhaps Figure 3.1 should be drawn as an expanding lens of a camera – moving out towards the world.

PHYSIOLOGICAL NEEDS

The concept of physiological drives has usually been taken as the starting point for motivational theory. Here Maslow advocated the use of the word *need* as an alternative to *drive*, basing his case on the notion of physical homeostasis, the body's natural effort to maintain a constant normal state of the bloodstream, coupled with the finding that appetites in the sense of preferential choices of food are a fairly efficient indicator of actual deficiencies in the body.

Not all physiological needs were homeostatic, for the list could be extended to include sexual desire, sleepiness, sheer activity and maternal behaviour in animals. Indeed, if a growing loss of specificity in description was acceptable, he held that it would be possible to extend the list of physiological needs very considerably.

For two reasons Maslow considered the physical needs to be unique rather than typical of the basic human needs:-

• They could be regarded as relatively independent of one another and other orders of needs.

- In the classic cases of hunger, thirst and sex, there was a localized physical base for the need.

Yet this relative uniqueness could not be equated with isolation: the physiological needs might serve as channels for all sorts of other needs as well. The man who thinks he is hungry, for example, may be looking for security rather than carbohydrates or proteins.

If a person becomes chronically short of food and water he becomes dominated by the desire to eat and to drink, and his concern for other needs tends to be swept away. Thus the physiological needs are the most prepotent of all needs. What this prepotence means precisely is that the human being who is missing everything in life in an extreme fashion will still tend to seek satisfaction for his physiological needs rather than any others. Under such temporary dominance a person's whole attitude to the future may undergo change: 'For our chronically and extremely hungry man, Utopia can be defined simply as a place where there is plenty of food . . . Such a man may fairly be said to live by bread alone.'

SAFETY NEEDS

When the physiological needs are relatively well satisfied, a new set of needs emerges centred upon the safety of the organism. Owing to the inhibition by adults of any signs of reaction to threat or danger this aspect of human behaviour is more easily observed in children, who react in a total manner to any sudden disturbance, such as being dropped, startled by loud noises, flashing lights, by rough handling, or by inadequate support.

Maslow found other indications for the need of safety in a child's preference for routine or rhythm, for a predictable and orderly world. Injustice, unfairness or lack of consistency in the parents seem to make a child feel anxious and unsafe. 'This attitude may be not so much because of the injustice as such or any particular pains involved; but rather because this treatment threatens to make the world look unreliable, or unsafe, or unpredictable.' The consensus of informed opinion held that children thrived best under a *limited* permissiveness, for they need an organized or structured world. The sight of strange, unfamiliar or uncontrollable objects, illness or death can elicit fear responses in children. 'Particularly at such times, the child's frantic clinging to his parents is eloquent testimony to their role as protectors (quite apart from their roles as food givers and love givers).'

WHO WAS MASLOW?

Abraham Maslow died in 1970, having spent most of his long working life as lecturer and professor in psychology at Brandeis University in the state of New York. From an intellectual standpoint, Maslow's most formative years were those he had spent in the late 1930s in New York, which was then, as he later declared, 'beyond a doubt, the centre of the psychological universe of that time.'

Besides the analytical school, Maslow also studied the two other incipient schools in the contemporary psychology of his day, which he named respectively the 'holistic' and the 'cultural'. The world *holism* (from the Greek word for whole) had been first introduced in 1926 by Jan Smuts in his seminal book *Holism and*

Evolution to describe 'the principle which makes for the origin and progress of wholes in the universe'. Maslow learnt the application of the holistic approach to psychology from prominent members of the *Gestalt* school. Later he believed that he had found a bridge between the holistic and analytic schools in the teachings of Kurt Goldstein, whose book *The Organism*, published in 1939, in particular exerted a profound and life-long influence on Maslow, giving him, for example, the term 'self-actualization'.

Apart from investigating the social and cultural aspects of psychology, primarily with the aid of the anthropologist Ruth Benedict, Maslow also made a short field study of the Northern Blackfoot Indians. In addition, he had numerous conversations with other anthropologists in New York in the 1930s, such as Margaret Mead.

In 1954, Maslow (by then at Brandeis University) published a volume of articles and papers, under the title *Motivation and Personality*. Maslow had planned this collection in advance to be a synthesis of the analytical, *Gestalt* and social anthropological schools, feeling that they were 'intrinsically related to each other, and that they were sub-aspects of a single, larger, encompassing whole'. He also hoped that together they would help to make 'more meaningful' his earlier work in experimental psychology. 'Furthermore,' he added, 'I felt they would enable me to serve better my humanistic aims.'

In adults we may observe expressions of the safety needs in the common desire for employment with security of tenure, pension, and insurance schemes, and the improvement of safety conditions at work. Another attempt to seek safety and stability in the world may be seen in the very common preference for familiar rather than unfamiliar things, or for the known rather than the unknown.

THE CASE OF THE BORN YACHTSMAN

Anthony Clark worked as a senior manager in a large insurance company. Having reached the age of fifty he decided to take the opportunity of early retirement. His two children had just completed university; the mortgage had been paid off and he had a good pension as well as an inheritance from his parents. His financial security was assured. As he told a friend, 'A satisfied need ceases to motivate, according to one of those management gurus, I can't remember his name. Can't see any reason now why I should carry on working until retirement age when I can do now the things I really want to do.'

He decided to study French and Spanish at the local university – he had a natural aptitude for languages which he had never been able to develop. He also loved sailing at weekends and he persuaded his wife into the idea of buying a small cruiser for coasting down France and Spain into the Mediterranean. He was doing what he found most fulfilling.

SOCIAL NEEDS

If the physiological and safety needs are met, Maslow suggested, then the needs for love, affection and belonging-ness will emerge as the dominant centre of motivation. The person concerned will feel keenly the absence of friends or family; he or she will strive for affectionate relations with people and for 'a place in the group'. We may best call this set the 'Social Needs'.

THE CASE OF THE MISSED FRIENDS

Wendy Hurst had trained as a nurse but she left in order to start a family. As the years went on she found she missed increasingly the social side of work and she told her husband that she intended to return to nursing, at first on a part-time basis until her youngest child had gone to secondary school and then full-time.

'But we don't need the extra money, Wendy,' said her husband Jack. 'But that's not the point,' she replied. 'I just know I would find it more interesting and stimulating to be working with people again. I really miss my friends. We used to have a lot of fun. I know I have some social life in the village here – and our family, of course, which will always come first – but it's not the same as being a member of a team.'

Social needs are intrinsic to our human nature. We are born into a small society – the family – and we become individuals. But we never lose our need for each other. Work, as Maslow suggests, does provide one important means by which this need within us is met. For work is a matrix of friendship and camaraderie.

EXERCISE

Make a list of three ways in which the following organizations meet the social needs of their staff members:

- a famous regiment
- a university department
- a charitable or voluntary organization known to you

- the organization in which you work now
- your old school

ESTEEM NEEDS

This category in Maslow's thought includes the need or desire both for a high evaluation of self (self-respect or self-esteem) and for the esteem of others. Maslow divided them into two subsidiary sets:

- the desire for strength, achievement, adequacy, mastery, competence, confidence in the face of the world, independence, and freedom; and
- the desire for reputation, prestige, status, dominance, recognition, attention, importance and appreciation.

From the old Greek idea of *hubris* (insolent or contemptuous pride) as well as from such sources as the writings of Eric Fromm, Maslow believed that 'we have been learning more and more of the dangers of basing self-esteem on the opinions of others rather than on real capacity, competence, and adequacy to the task. The most stable and therefore most healthy self-esteem is based on *deserved* respect from others rather than on external fame or celebrity and unwarranted adulation.'

THE CASE OF THE DISGRUNTLED PRODUCER

Brian Glanville is head of English and Drama in a large comprehensive school. Each year he produces and directs a major school play. 'It's an enormous effort', he explained, 'and, of course, each year you put your reputation on the line.

But one thing that really made it worthwhile for me is that afterwards at the weekly staff meeting the Head always said some complimentary things about the play and my contribution. That is, until this year,' he added.

'Why was it different this year?' I inquired, noticing his rather crestfallen look.

'Well, he is leaving at the end of the year and he has totally lost interest. At the first staff meeting after the play – an especially difficult one to turn into such a success because we really didn't have much acting talent – he said absolutely nothing. I was so pissed off that at the end of the meeting I said, "I want to thank everyone who helped to make the play a success" and then walked out. He gave me no recognition at all.'

THE NEED FOR SELF-ACTUALIZATION

'Even if all these needs are satisfied,' wrote Maslow, 'we may still often (if not always) expect that a new discontent and restlessness will soon develop, unless the individual is doing what he is fitted for. A musician must make music, an artist must paint, a poet must write, if he is to be ultimately at peace with himself. What a man *can* be, he *must* be. This need we may call self-actualization.'

Maslow defined self-actualization as 'man's desire for self-fulfilment, namely, to the tendency for him to become actualized in what he is potentially . . . the desire to become more and more what one is, to become everything that one is capable of becoming. The clear emergence of these needs usually rests upon prior satisfaction of the physiological, safety, love and esteeem needs.'

THE CASE OF SANDRA JOLLY

Is there a universal human need or urge to actualize or fulfil the human potential – both general and special-talent – in all of us? There is a broad case for believing so. Is it more conscious in women than in men? Sandra Jolly was a very talented cellist, but she felt strongly the need to fulfil herself as a person and as a woman. In her case that led her into a relationship with a fellow musician which she found fulfilling. When their first child arrived she felt that she had found an even deeper self-fulfilment as a mother. Although she was painfully conscious of a real sacrifice in her career – she could not maintain her position as a world-class cellist in those vital years – she valued more highly her fulfilment within a pattern of loving relationships. Her equally gifted best friend, a violinist, had made the opposite choice: giving up the possibility of a marriage and a family in order to pursue single-mindedly her passion for beauty in music.

Maslow called this above set of needs the CONATIVE needs, those dealing with willing or desiring. It is worth adding that Maslow also sketched out – much more lightly – two other related families of need which he called the COGNITIVE needs (the needs to know and understand) and the AESTHETIC needs (the needs for beauty). You may notice, if you read his book, that there is some ambiguity about Maslow's language at this point. When he writes about 'higher needs' he is sometimes referring to esteem and self-actualization; at other times, however, he has in mind the cognitive and aesthetic needs.

Again values come into the story here. Just as the conative needs form a stairway of desires leading up to what Maslow regarded as the supreme GOOD for humanity (the state of self-actualization) so his cognitive needs can be interpreted as steps leading to TRUTH and the aesthetic needs as those ascending to BEAUTY. These three suns shine and draw us, though their light is filtered and refracted by the clouds of cultures that move across our personal sky. Of course, whether there are such meta-values as Goodness, Truth and Beauty 'out there', so to speak independent of the human mind, is a matter of philosophical opinion. It is not irrational to believe that it might be so. Plato certainly believed it. So do some great religions. Be that as it may, certainly holding that goodness, truth and beauty do have a reality apart from any individual's subjective perception of them has proved to be a productive hypothesis for humanity in a variety of ways.

KEY POINTS ON MASLOW

Maslow's hierarchy of needs has become so universal that it's often taught at second or third hand from summaries of his work and distortions inevitably creep in. It is now possible to see his theory in its historical perspective. Here are the key points:

- Although common sense and experience do lend some support to the principle that 'a satisfied need ceases to motivate', there is not convincing evidence that the satisfaction of any one need on Maslow's hierarchy will lead to its upper neighbour becoming the next prime motive. If your social needs are met you don't move on to the esteem needs.
- Our physiological and security needs are more basic (we share them with animals). If they are threatened we jump

down the ladder and defend. The higher needs in the conative hierarchy are weaker, but they are more distinctively human: they make us persons. Indeed Maslow equates self-actualization with psychological health or full humanity.

- While the needs can be considered as a loose, step-wise progression, Maslow held that it was possible for higher level needs to emerge at some point prior to the total satisfaction of the lower-level needs.

- Factors such as culture and the age of the person will clearly affect the value or weight given to the needs that Maslow discerned.

- The fact that several studies of the available research findings on motivation have found no support for Maslow's theory to any significant degree doesn't imply that it was wrong but merely that it was not supported.

- Many people show a willingness to go without the more basic needs in order to meet their needs for achievement, recognition and fulfilment.

CONCLUSION

Maslow's theory has an inherent appeal and obvious relevance for managers. It is widely used for explaining why different needs and motives may be expected to operate in different situations. It has some limited value for prognosis: *when* this set of conditions happens, *then* this or that factor will become important.

It has been described as an *on-the-average* theory. The general deduction most often drawn from it as a universal rule of thumb is that 'employees may be expected to want more'. That generalization overlooks the point that the 'more' people want will be qualitatively different from what they have received in the past.

Despite the fact that Maslow was so preoccupied with the individual, the theory – as understood by many managers – doesn't stress individual differences or suggest the idea that each person will have a unique set of needs and values. Rather it induces in them the *on-the-average* way of thinking about individuals rather than groups.

Yet the five sets of need in the hierarchy still serve a most useful purpose. Together they form a sketch map – no more – of individual needs for you to consider as a leader in relation to each member of your team. In the context of the more general three-circles model of needs at work (see Chapter Eight), as we shall see, they make their fullest sense.

'Such is the state of life that none are happy but by the anticipation of change. The change itself is nothing; when we have made it, the next wish is to change again.'

Samuel Johnson

4

NOT FOR BREAD ALONE

Perhaps the most complex, confused and controversial aspect of Maslow's thought is its central concept — self-actualization. He borrowed the term from Kurt Goldstein, a pioneer in the American school of humanistic psychology. It's a synonym for self-realization or self-fulfilment.

It is a complex matter because, as Maslow himself became aware, the term *self-actualization* is misleading in several respects. It's confusing because Maslow himself was confused about it. And it's controversial because by no means everyone believes that work should be structured or arranged to allow for self-actualization, whatever it may be.

It is tempting to drop the subject from this book, but I believe that would be a mistake. For Maslow was groping towards seeing a strand in what motivates humans to work that is going to be immensely important in the world during the next century. It may be so to you already.

MASLOW ON SELF-ACTUALIZATION

Let's start by trying to unravel what Maslow meant by self-actualization. Two senses in which he uses the term can be distinguished:

Particular	a drive in a creative artist or anyone else aware of possessing special talent, ability or gift to use and develop this to the full.
General	a universal urge in any person to grow and develop as a full human person, realizing all the distinctively human potentials within us.

Now Maslow equated self-actualization in this second sense with what he called psychological health. In another paper, entitled, 'Self-Actualizing People: A Study in Psychological Health', he attempted to characterize or paint a portrait of 'self-actualizing people'. His definition of the criteria he used for selecting his handful of subjects, apart from their freedom from personality disorders, reveals again his confusion of the particular and general definitions.

'the full use and exploitation of talents, capacities, potentialities, etc. . . . They are people who have developed or are developing to the full stature of which they are capable. These potentialities may be either idiosyncratic or species-wide, so that the self in self-actualization must not have too individualistic a flavour.'

His list of cases, partial cases and potential or possible cases included creative artists such as Beethoven, Goethe,

Walt Whitman, Henry Thoreau and the violinist Fritz Kreisler on the one hand and more general or representative human figures on the other hand, such as Thomas Jefferson, Abraham Lincoln, Eleanor Roosevelt, Albert Schweitzer and philosopher Spinoza.

What can we make of all this? Maslow's portrait of self-actualizing or psychologically healthy people (for which he claimed no scientific authority) is really a portrait of *goodness*. I will not enumerate here his eighteen characteristics or components of goodness (*alias* health), for I have done so in *Understanding Motivation* (1989), a specialist study of his work (see *Further Reading*). His list includes – not surprisingly considering his subjects – a number of characteristics associated with creative people. The difficulty is that we would be moving away from description and into the realm of value judgements – however disguised by such labels as 'self-actualization' or 'maturity' or 'psychological health'. What is good for us and what constitutes a good person are philosophical questions which admit to a variety of answers.

The isthmus between the narrower and wider aspects of self-actualization comes in Maslow's fourteenth characteristic, which he called *creativeness*.

'This is a universal characteristic of all the people studied or observed,' declared Maslow. 'There is no exception. Each one shows in one way or another a special kind of creativeness or originality or inventiveness that has certain characteristics.' In contrast to the 'special-talent' creativeness of a Mozart these people display a general creativeness akin to that which is evident in children. It bestows upon all they do a certain attitude or spirit: 'In this sense there can be creative shoemakers or carpenters or clerks.' Maslow believed that powerful sets of inhibitions normally damped down this natural spontaneity which reappeared in self-actualizing people. 'Perhaps when we speak of creativeness here we are simply describing from another point of view, namely, from the point of view of consequence, what we have described above as a greater freshness, penetration, and efficiency of perception.'

The first clue, then, lies in this broad-brush idea of an inherent *creativity* in human nature, which will emerge or find expression when the other areas of need have been met.

The second clue is to be found in the concept of *growth*. The word *holistic* comes from *holism*, which was invented by Field Marshal Jan Smuts of South Africa in 1927 to describe the process whereby nature aggregates parts into wholes organically. A baby is a whole that grows larger. In the course of time holistic came to be used as a general description for the school of philosophy that Maslow epitomises.

DISINFECTING SELF-ACTUALIZATION FROM EGOISM

Having saddled himself with the phrase self-actualization as his distinctive message, Maslow did his best to empty its saddlebags of misleading luggage.

The first problem is that in English *self*-actualization sounds close to *self*-centredness, if not to selfishness. Maslow tried hard to distinguish proper self-interest in your own welfare and happiness from a selfish preoccupation with one's own salvation at all costs or by any route.

Maslow's route out of that impasse was to stress how other-centred his subjects were, how much they gave themselves to worthwhile purposes without thought of themselves, how clear it was that their self-actualization was a by-product of what he confusingly called 'self-actualizing work'. He never wearied from repeating the paradox that in the self-actualized person the dichotomy between selfishness and unselfishness has been transcended. The self-actualizers are unselfish and other-centred, but they also possess a healthy regard for themselves, perhaps more than that of most people.

Eventually Maslow came to see that the phrase 'self-actualization' itself presented a stumbling block which no amount of explanation could quite overcome: 'Besides being clumsy from a literary point of view,' he wrote, 'this term has proven to have the unforeseen shortcomings of appearing:

- to imply selfishness rather than altruism;
- to slur the aspect of duty and of dedication to life's tasks;
- to neglect the ties to other people and to society, and the dependence of individual fulfilment upon a "good society";
- to neglect egolessness and self-transcendence; and
- to stress, by implication, activity rather than passivity or receptivity.

'This has turned out to be so in spite of my careful efforts to describe the empirical *fact* that self-actualizing people are altruistic, dedicated, self-transcending, and social.'

A JOURNEY NOT A DESTINATION

The misleading luggage in the other saddlebag of self-actualization is the nuance that it is an end-state. Some have arrived, others haven't. The former have achieved fully their psychological health as humans; they are fully mature. For them work now becomes a means of expressing their self-fulfilment, not a way of attaining it.

Unfortunately this sort of assumption strikes no musical chords of response in the human spirit.

The metaphor behind the phrase self-fulfilment is the self as being like an empty container which is filled up or made full: having within its limits all it will hold, no space being empty. In some ways it isn't a very happy idea because a full glass means that the process of filling (living?) is complete or has come to an end. What's the point of pouring more wine into a glass that is full? We all know what happens to plants that have finished growing! But human lives, as it has been said about books, are never finished — only abandoned. As the proverb says, 'Leave endings to God.'

> This is Your Life
>
> 'I ain't what I ought to be
> I ain't what I'm going to be
> But I ain't what I was!'
>
> *Anon. graffiti in an Arizonan bar*

There is a legend that Alexander the Great was once found weeping because — at the age of thirty — he had no more worlds to conquer. Most people are Alexanders in this respect. The Alexander Principle, as I call it, is that we all need new worlds to conquer. The organic analogy of growing does apply to us in some obvious way but — like all analogies — it breaks down at some point, or at least we may hope it does. Our spirits abhor the notion of a final station stop, labelled self-actualization, maturity or psychological health. As Meister Eckhart, the fourteenth-century German mystic, wrote: 'There is no stopping place in this life. No, nor was there ever one for anyone – no matter how far along the way they have come. This then, above all things: be ready for the gifts of God and always for new ones.'

HUMAN CREATIVITY

In the light of these overtures, it makes sense to talk about work as being relatively *fulfilling* or not. We can make an immediate distinction here between work and drudgery or labour.

Incidentally, management thinkers like Maslow, Frederick Herzberg and Douglas McGregor were fond of grounding their ideas in the Bible. In fact it was St Augustine who first made the distinction between work and toil. Work was the natural state of Adam (which is the Hebrew word for Man). The essence of the manager's vocation is to bring order out of chaos. That is the task that was assigned to Adam. Only as a result of the 'Fall' did work turn into labour. The creation story included, then, an attempt to 'explain' the present back-breaking toil in the stony fields of Israel, as witnessed by the Biblical writers, in terms of a spiritual cause. The restoration of humanity by a new infusion of the divine spirit would entail that work would recover its lost original meaning.

What kind of work did Maslow have in mind? Can we identify the elements in work (as opposed to the tread-mill or slave galley) that make it at least potentially *fulfilling?* Maslow's own description in *The Farther Reaches of Human Nature* includes one clue worth following up:

'Self-actualizing people are, without one single exception, involved in a cause outside their own skin, in something outside of themselves. They are devoted, working at something, something which is very precious to them – some calling or vocation in the old sense, the priestly sense. They are working at something which fate has called them to somehow and which they work at and which they love, so that the work-joy dichotomy in them disappears. All, in one way or another, devote their lives to the search of what I have called the "being" values, the ultimate values which are intrinsic, which cannot be reduced to anything more ultimate.'

The clue in question is that word *vocation*. Set aside in this context the issue of who or what 'calls' anyone to a particular line of work. Focus instead upon the characteristics of vocational work. Those with a sense of vocation tend to be involved in *creative* work or in work that is primarily of *service* to others. Of course these two major categories are not exclusive.

EINSTEIN'S OTHER THEORY

Well-being and happiness never appeared to me to be absolute aims. I am more inclined to compare such moral aims to the ambitions of a pig. Only a life lived for others is worth living.

The difficulty of this line of thought is that *creativeness*, it is assumed, was a gift or talent entrusted to the happy few – the Einsteins, Leonardo da Vincis and Mozarts of this world. The critical issue is FEW or MANY? One influential thinker, Douglas McGregor, boldly argued that what was thought to be the possession of the FEW was actually present in the MANY – including you and me. And, moreover, it was feasible for industry to accommodate and profit from this widespread, if not universal, human *creativity* in us all.

THEORY X AND THEORY Y

WHO WAS DOUGLAS McGREGOR?

Born in Detroit in 1906, the son of a Presbyterian minister, McGregor graduated at Wayne University and worked as a social psychologist at Harvard University before becoming a professor at the Massachusetts Institute of Technology. As a management consultant he worked with Standard Oil of New Jersey, Bell Telephone, Union Carbide and Imperial Chemical Industries (UK). He had a spell of six years as President of Antioch College in Ohio but returned to MIT. He was killed in a car accident in 1962.

EXERCISE

Check through the following nine propositions and tick in the appropriate box whether you agree or disagree with them.

	Yes	No
(1) The average human being has an inherent dislike of work and will avoid it if he can.	☐	☐

(2) Because of this human characteristic dislike of work, most people must be coerced, controlled, directed, threatened with punishment to get them to put forth adequate effort toward the achievement of organizational objectives. ❑ ❑

(3) The average human being prefers to be directed, wishes to avoid responsibility, has relatively little ambition, and wants security above all. ❑ ❑

(4) The expenditure of physical and mental effort in work is as natural as play or rest. ❑ ❑

(5) External control and the threat of punishment are not the only means for bringing about effort toward organizational objectives. Man will exercise self-direction and self-control in the service of objectives to which he is committed. ❑ ❑

(6) Commitment to objectives is a function of the rewards associated with their achievement. ❑ ❑

(7) The average human being learns, under proper conditions, not only to accept but to seek responsibility. ❑ ❑

(8) The capacity to exercise a relatively high degree of imagination, ingenuity, and creativity in the solution of organizational problems is widely, not narrowly, distributed in the population. ❑ ❑

(9) Under the conditions of modern industrial life, the intellectual potentialities of the average human being are only partially utilized. ❑ ❑

You may like to repeat this exercise now with the management of your present organization in mind. Judging their attitudes and actions (leave aside what they say or profess in the company mission statement), do you think they show agreement or disagreement with each of these basic propositions?

The first three principles listed in the above Exercise are those that McGregor grouped together as Theory X. It was, he said, the traditional view of direction and control. Those who believe – consciously or unconsciously – in Theory X assume that people have little or no interest in the organization in which they work or its common purpose. They are driven by fear or threats or lured by the financial inducements on offer – the 'stick-and-carrot' approach.

FIRST-LINE BOSSES

'In the American factory at the turn of the century, the foreman had primary responsibility for implementing management's goals; he was the "undisputed ruler of his department, gang, crew, or ship".

When in 1912 a congressional committee investigated the United States Steel Corporation, they attempted to understand just how the foreman functioned. They learned that foremen throughout American industry practised something known as "the driving method", an approach to supervision that combined authoritarian combativeness with physical intimidation in order to extract the maximum effort from the worker.

The driving method was well suited to work that depended upon the consistent exertion of the human body. The foreman's profanity, threats, and punishments were complemented by the workers' methods for limiting output.'

From Shoshana Zuboff, *In the Age of the Smart Machine: The Future of Work and Power* (1988)

By contrast, the remaining six propositions – Theory Y – imply a level of integration between individual and organizational goals. We could make the point visually thus:

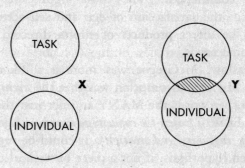

Figure 4.1   Theory X and Theory Y

Where the two circles don't overlap at all you will find alienation. The shaded portion where the task and individual circles are perceived by both the company and the individual to overlap suggests a very different kind of relationship. It is more akin to a form of partnership. That doesn't mean that there are no *tensions* between individual needs and the requirements of the task, but there is no essential *conflict*. Both parties can work together to achieve an acceptable balance between their distinct but overlapping and therefore mutual interests.

Now McGregor has drawn heavily upon the work of Maslow: indeed, if one subtracts the Maslow-inspired passages there is not much left of Theory Y. McGregor had swallowed Maslow's theory of a hierarchy of needs hook, line and sinker, but he digested it into language which industrial and commercial managers could understand. Moreover, he integrated the theory with the more traditional preoccupations of management by suggesting that the needs of the individual and the needs of the organization were not inherently incompatible. Under the third proposition above in the Theory Y cluster, for example, McGregor commented: 'The most significant of such rewards, e.g. the satisfaction of ego and self-actualization needs, can be direct products of efforts directed towards organizational needs.'

Like Maslow, McGregor was more a thinker than a researcher. His core assumption was that the *average human being* – in other words the MANY and not just the elite or privileged FEW – *possess the capacity to exercise a high degree of imagination, ingenuity and creativity*. It could be regarded as an unproven hypothesis, if not a piece of wishful thinking. It remained for the third person in the trinity of motivational theorists – Frederick Herzberg – to try to demonstrate with empirical research that McGregor's hypothesis was correct. To that attempt we turn in the next two chapters.

SERVING OTHERS

You may have noticed that McGregor and (as we shall see) Herzberg homed in on one aspect of vocational work (the kind of work associated with fulfilment), namely, the creative aspect. They suggested that the urge or desire to create was much more widespread than previously had been imagined. But what about that other facet or dimension – service to others? That aspect received no attention. Yet, paradoxically, it may prove to be even more important in the long run than the capacity to create. At the core of organizational tasks today lies the *customer service* demand. That applies, of course, to customers within the organization as well as those outside it. It will call eventually for a much higher level of service than is normal today. Thus the spirit of service may well come much more to the fore. It's the new frontier in motivational development for the next century.

THE CALL TO SERVE NEIGHBOUR THROUGH WORK

The first person to revolutionize the modern understanding of work was Martin Luther. He extended the concept of vocation from the FEW (priests, monks and nuns) to the MANY – all men and women in the double callings of work and marriage. The layman loved his neighbour *through* his work – not by abandoning it to live idly in a monastery. Listen to Luther preaching his message to a packed church in Wittenberg one Sunday morning in 1520:

'To use a rough example: If you are a craftsman you will find the Bible placed in your workshop, in your hands, in your hearts; it teaches and preaches how you ought to treat your neigbour. Only look at your tools, your needle, your thimble, your beer barrel, your articles of trade, your scales, your measures, and you will find this saying written on them. You will not be able to look anywhere where it does not strike your eyes. None of the things with which you deal daily are too trifling to tell you this incessantly, if you are but willing to hear it; and there is no lack of such preaching, for you have as many preachers as there are transactions, commodities, tools, and other implements in your house and estate; and they shout this to your face. "My dear, use me toward your neighbour as you would want him to act toward you with that which is his".'

Notice the principle of reciprocity. Give the same quality of goods and service to others as you want them to give to you through their trades and professions. In this way the faithful worker, Luther taught, becomes a conduit of God's love to his or her neighbour. And work is thus transformed into service.

Whether they have a *creative* or *service* dimension (or both), worthwhile tasks are the whetstones upon which talent is sharpened. Talent, however, has a more general meaning. It comes from the Biblical story of the man travelling to a far country who entrusted five talents – specific weights of gold or silver in the ancient world – to one of his servants, two to another and one to yet another, 'to every man according to his own ability'. The latter servant decided to play safe and buried his talent, whereas his two colleagues took some risks and doubled the talents entrusted to them.

They were rewarded by their master on his homecoming with recognition – 'Well done, you good and faithful servant' and given greater responsibilities, whereas the cautious steward found himself in big trouble. He rationalized his lack of motivation by saying 'Lord, I knew that you are a hard man, reaping where you have not sown and gathering where you have not strawed, and so I was afraid and hid your talent in the earth. Here you are, you have back what is your own.' His master condemned him for his slothful inaction – why didn't you put it in the bank and get some interest? – and punished him.

Your talents, however, are not gold or silver bars as in the story, but your *natural* abilities or aptitudes. They give you a capacity for success in some department of mental or physical activity. Therefore talents are not confined to the creative domain: you can have a talent for selling, repairing engines, finance, administration, design or gardening. *EVERYONE IS A POTENTIAL SUCCESS AT SOMETHING.*

CONCLUSION

The seeds of the future lie in the present. As far as practical management is concerned, if Douglas McGregor is right then there are still immense untapped resources of goodwill, energy, creativity and intelligence in people in employment today – and those who, through no fault of their own, are unemployed.

Personally I believe that the quality movement, initiated in Japan but now universal, has proved that McGregor was indeed right. But human creativity is now much more a team effort. The old individualistic models of painter or author, composer or sculptor, are not so relevant to us. Nor, incidentally, is the individualistic pattern of direct personal service – such as nurse-to-patient, teacher-to-pupil – the sole one. We serve society as much as individuals. Our service is rendered in teams or organizations, not on a one-to-one basis. The issue is whether or not the spirit of love which inspirited the FEW can now animate the MANY. The signs are promising, given good leadership.

> *It were no slight attainment could we merely*
> *fulfil what the nature of man implies.*
>
> > *Epictetus*

5

THE HYGIENE FACTORS

'Job satisfaction' is a common phrase these days. It stems directly or indirectly from the influential motivational research of another American professor of psychology, Frederick Herzberg. Although much controversy surrounds his ideas he made an important and influential contribution to our understanding of motivation at work.

In essence Herzberg made two claims. First, he said that he had found evidence through studying the components of *job satisfaction* that people were in fact motivated by such 'higher' needs as achievement, recognition and self-actualization. Secondly, he claimed that a practical programme of *job enrichment* in industry and commerce would create more job satisfaction by strengthening what he called the 'motivators'. This recipe for change would, he said, not only make for human happiness but also save industry some money. For a major problem in industry in the 1960s and 1970s – when Herzberg's work flourished – was the high labour turnover. A job-satisfied staff would stay longer.

Notice at the outset that the concepts of satisfaction and motivation are not the same, despite some overlap. You can be satisfied with a job – or relatively satisfied – without being much motivated.

Some friends thought that Maureen's job at the local supermarket, working as a check-out desk assistant, was too low-grade for a person of her qualifications and ability. She was not enthusiastic about her work either, but very satisfied with the job. 'It pays well,' she explained to them, 'and I can be home in time to get tea for the children. There's a good lot of girls working there. And we get a 10 percent discount on anything we buy for ourselves.'

As I mentioned, Herzberg labelled the factors that lead to high job satisfaction as the 'motivators'. That brings his work very much into our field of interest. Moreover, along with Maslow's 'hierarchy of needs', Herzberg's 'motivation-hygiene theory' has become part of the mainstream tradition in management thought. What can you learn from it? Before seeking to answer that question, why not subject yourself to his test?

EXERCISE

Here is a list of factors that may affect your attitude to your job. Please rank them in order of their importance to you personally. There can be no ties.

In ranking these factors, put 1 against the factor that is most important to you, 2 against the next and so on to 15.

When you have rated the factors in order of importance to yourself, please consider the order in which a representative member of your work team would rate them. Complete the second column as you think a typical subordinate would.

YOU		SUBORDINATE
☐	Achievement	☐
☐	Advancement	☐
☐	Company policy and administration	☐
☐	Job – possibility of individual growth	☐
☐	Job interest	☐
☐	Personal relationships – with Superiors	☐
☐	Personal relationships – with Colleagues	☐
☐	Personal relationships – with Subordinates	☐
☐	Personal life (factors outside work)	☐
☐	Recognition for effective work	☐
☐	Responsibility	☐
☐	Salary	☐
☐	Security	☐
☐	Status	☐
☐	Working conditions – physical	☐

HERZBERG'S RESEARCH STUDY

In 1959 Herzberg published his research into job attitudes in a book entitled *The Motivation to Work*. At the time of writing Herzberg, later Professor of Psychology at Western Reserve University, was Research Director at the Psychological Service of Pittsburgh. His co-authors, Bernard Mausner and Barbara Snyderman, were respectively Research Psychologist and Research Associate at the same institute.

With two other psychologists Herzberg and Mausner had carried out an earlier preliminary survey of the existing literature on the factors involved in attitudes to work. Despite differences in content and methods in the 155 books and articles they considered, Herzberg and his colleagues felt able to draw a major conclusion:

> 'The one dramatic finding that emerged in our review of this literature was the fact that there was a difference in the primacy of factors, depending upon whether the investigator was looking for things the worker liked about his job or things he disliked. The concept that there were some factors that were 'satisfiers' and others that were 'dissatisfiers' was suggested by this finding. From it was derived one of the basic hypotheses of our own study.'

After two pilot schemes, involving respectively thirteen labourers, clerical workers, foremen, plant engineers and accountants, and thirty-nine middle-managers (all but six of them engineers of one kind or another), the research team launched into a study of the job attitudes of 203 engineers and accountants working in nine factories or plants around

Pittsburgh. The description and discussion of this particular research project formed the main content of *The Motivation to Work*. Moreover, the research served as a model for many replications in the next decade. Consequently it is important to grasp the essential research Herzberg and his colleagues undertook. Owing to the style of the writers this is not an easy task, but we can distinguish three major characteristics:

- **Specification of Experience**
  Each of the 203 subjects was asked to identify periods in their own history when their feelings about their jobs were markedly either higher or lower than usual. The researcher made the assumption that the respondents would be able to recognize the extremes of this continuum of feelings and to select extreme situations to report. They distinguished between short and long-term sequences of events, but in each case the 'story' had to be finite in terms of having a beginning, middle and end.
- **Factors-Attitudes-Effects**
  The research aimed at unravelling the inter-relations between objective 'events' in the historical accounts, coupled with the feelings which were expressed about them by the subjects, and the effects which resulted. Rather confusingly, the reported events were labelled 'first-level factors' and the allied feelings 'second-level factors', while the word 'factor' was also used about the combinations of both together. The word 'attitude' means in this context the more settled or habitual mode of regarding aspects of life. 'Effects' included job performance (based on the subject's own reports of quantifiable or qualitative changes), mental health, inter-personal

relationships, attitude towards the company and other attitudes allied to the working situation.

- **Research Methods**

The researchers employed the technique of the 'semi-structured' interview, in which the interviewer asks some pre-arranged questions but has freedom to pursue any lines of inquiry that he judges might be fruitful. 'The questions were so designed that for each story we were sure to get the factors-attitudes-effects information for which we sought.' Each respondent could choose a story about a time when he felt exceptionally good or exceptionally bad about the job. After this sequence had been thoroughly discussed and analyzed, the interviewer asked for a second story, which had to be opposite in terms of good/bad and short/long range sequence of events from the first one. Some respondents volunteered a third or fourth story.

The researchers attempted to set up categories of factors and effects from the material gathered. Carefully cross-checking one another's judgements, the team broke down the replies into 'thought units' – defined as 'a statement about a single event or condition that led to a feeling, a single characterization of a feeling, or a description of a single effect', e.g. the statement 'The way it was given to me showed the supervisor had confidence in my work.' A sample of 5,000 'thought units' of the entire (unspecified) total was sorted out into three major categories: first-level factors, second-level factors and effects. Each of these main ones was further sub-divided into lesser categories. Once ninety-five per cent agreement among them on the categories had been achieved, the research team proceeded to analyze 476 stories or 'sequences of events'.

The research team's first-level factors — fourteen categories of elements or acts in the situation which the respondents found to be sources of good or bad feelings — were as follows:

- Recognition
- Achievement
- Possibility of growth
- Advancement
- Salary
- Interpersonal relations
- Supervision – technical
- Responsibility
- Company policy and administration
- Working conditions
- Work itself
- Factors in personal life
- Status
- Job security

Under the heading of 'Second Level Factors' the researchers analyzed the responses of the interviewee to the question, 'What did these events mean to you?' Naturally the information at this point was limited by the extent to which the respondents could articulate their feelings and the level of insight which enabled them to report real perceptions rather than stereotyped reactions based on socially accepted ideas. These second-level inferences or generalizations were therefore to be distinguished from the statements of feeling in the verbal responses of the 'first-level' factors. The eleven second-level factors or clusters of feelings share for the most part the same names as the first-level ones; for example: recognition, achievement, possible growth, responsibility, belonging and interest. 'Feelings about salary' was included to cover those situations in which 'the first-level factor was viewed primarily as a source of the things that money can bring. If an answer to the question, "Why did this promotion make you feel good?" was, "I like the idea of being able to make more money", then the second-level factor was coded "salary".'

The analysis of '*effects*' into categories posed fewer problems, because most respondents were specific and concrete in their replies:

Performance effects	This major category included three sub-categories. The first consisted of general comments about work being better or worse than usual; the second embraced comments about the rate of work; and in the third were mustered remarks concerning the quality of work.
Turnover	At one end of the 'turnover' continuum the respondent actually resigned or left his job; at the other his positive feelings about his work and the company had mounted so considerably that he turned down attractive offers to go elsewhere.
Mental health	Positive statements included a lessening of tension symptoms, gaining weight when underweight, and stopping too much drinking or smoking. The more numerous negative reports, however, mentioned psychomatic effects (skin disorders, ulcers, heart condition), physiological changes related to tensions (such as severe headaches and loss of appetite), and more

	diffuse symptoms of anxiety possibly related to temperamental dispositions in the individual.
Interpersonal relations	There were many instances where the job had appeared to influence for better or worse a man's relationships with his family.
Additional	Respondents also reported changed attitudes towards themselves, their colleagues, their professions or the companies which employed them.

WHAT CAUSES JOB DISSATISFACTION?

The major question that the members of the research team had posed themselves was whether or not different kinds of factors brought about job satisfaction and job dissatisfaction. A number of minor questions which interested them related to the correlations between the variables of long-term and short-term sequences, first-level and second-level factors, effects and attitudes, profession, education, job level and experience. Broadly speaking, the team felt convinced that their main hypothesis – that there *were* two distinct sets of factors involved – had been justified by the study.

'The factors that are rarely instrumental in bringing about high job attitudes focus not on the job itself but rather on the characteristics of the context in which the job is done: working conditions, inter-personal relationships, supervision, company policies, administration of these policies, effects on the worker's personal life, job security, and salary. This is a basic distinction. The satisfiers relate to the *actual job*. Those factors that do not act as satisfiers describe the *job situation*.'

For the complex of factors which describe the *surrounds* of the job and can cause discontent, Herzberg recruited the word *hygiene* from the medical world. 'Hygiene operates to remove health hazards from the environment of man. It is not a curative; it is, rather, a preventive. Modern garbage disposal, water purification, and air-pollution do not cure diseases, but without them we would have more diseases.'

HYGIENE FACTORS	
Company policy and administration	Availability of clearly defined policies, especially those relating to people; adequacy of organization and management.
Supervision – technical	Accessibility, competence and fairness of your superior.
Interpersonal relations	The relations with supervisors, subordinates and colleagues; the quality of social life at work
Salary	The total compensation package, such as wages, salary, pension, company car and other financially related benefits.
Status	A person's position or rank in relation to others, symbolized by title, parking space, car, size of offices, furnishings.
Job security	Freedom from insecurity, such as loss of position or loss of employment altogether.

HYGIENE FACTORS (Cont)	
Personal life	The effect of a person's work on family life, e.g. stress, unsocial hours or moving house
Working conditions	The physical conditions in which you work; the amount of work, facilities available, ventilation, tools, space, noise and other environmental aspects

Figure 5.1   Factors that Create Job Dissatisfaction

These are all the factors or elements in your work, according to Herzberg, that can make you feel unhappy or dissatisfied when you are at work.

EXERCISE

Can you think of three stories or incidents in your working life in the past nine months when you felt angry, frustrated or annoyed? Write them down briefly. Do they fall into any of the above categories? If not, invent another category of your own – the ninth hygiene factor.

CONCLUSION

In London during the 1970s I can recall attending one of Frederick Herzberg's crowded seminars and meeting him afterwards. There could be no doubt about his own enthusiasm for his message and commitment: one of the first of the great management gurus of our time.

Whether or not he was right about all the hygiene factors – especially salary – remains to be seen. But his general point that there are factors *around* the job which can cause dissatisfaction if they are not right, but have weak power as positive motivators, seems to me to be well-founded. I have known low morale in situations where all the comforts of modern life are available. Conversely, I have seen very high morale when working conditions were unavoidably awful.

Your responsibilities as a managerial leader include ensuring that the hygiene factors are met. That will not guarantee you success, but the neglect of them would be likely to result in a lack of success. Before reading on you may like to complete the checklist. Just to make doubly sure, why not photocopy it first and give it to your team?

CHECKLIST: HYGIENE FACTORS IN YOUR ORGANIZATION

	Yes	No
Is the working environment clean and pleasant?	❏	❏
Are noise levels acceptable?	❏	❏
Is the health and safety record exceptionally good?	❏	❏
Is smoking allowed in the buildings?	❏	❏
Do people have the proper tools and equipment to do their jobs?	❏	❏
Are the social and welfare amenities good?	❏	❏

CHECKLIST: HYGIENE FACTORS IN YOUR ORGANIZATION (Cont)

	Yes	No
Have poorly managed changes of organization induced personal stress?	❑	❑
Are there too many people on short-term contracts?	❑	❑
Have steps been taken to improve everyone's employability?	❑	❑
Are salaries and other rewards perceived to be fair?	❑	❑
Is there an 'us' and 'them' division between management and staff?	❑	❑
Has anyone lost status in the last six months by a downwards change of job title?	❑	❑

6

THE MOTIVATORS

Work is not the curse, but drudgery is.
Henry Ward Beecher

Next, Herzberg and his colleagues turned to the *motivators*. Heading the list of these 'satisfiers' are *achievement* and *recognition*, followed by *work itself, responsibility, advancement* and the *possibility of growth*. By reviewing all the variables the team suggested that the complex or cluster of *achievement-recognition-responsibility-work itself-advancement* are highly interrelated in both the short and long terms. 'When some or all of the factors are present in the job situation of an individual, the fulfilment of his basic needs is such that he enters a period of exceptionally positive feelings about his job.' For situational, professional or personal reasons the relative strengths of factors may vary, but the complex as a whole will always characterize job satisfaction.

WHAT MOTIVATES YOU

Visually the discontinuity between the 'satisfiers' and 'dissatisfiers' and their relative longevity could be shown by means of a diagram. Below I have reproduced Herzberg's original diagram or model from *The Motivation to Work* (1959). This is his description of it:

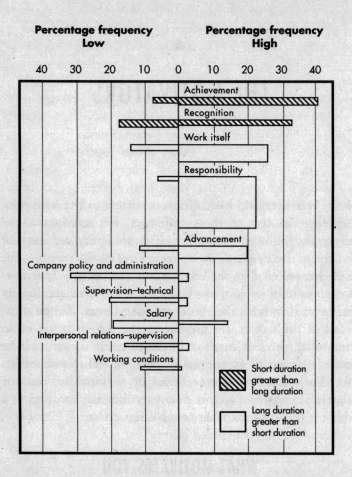

Figure 6.1 Comparison of satisfiers and dissatisfiers (203 Pittsburgh engineers and accountants). From *The Motivation to Work* (1959)

As indicated in the legend of this figure, the distance from the neutral area shows the percentage frequency with which each factor occurred in the high job-attitude sequences and in the low job-attitude sequences. The width of the boxes represents the ratio of long-range to short-range attitude effects; the wider the box, the more frequently this factor led to a long-range job attitude change. The factors of recognition and achievement are shaded in this figure to indicate that the width of their boxes portrays a reversal in the long-range ratio. The attitude effects of both these factors were substantially more short range.

The frequency and duration of *work itself, responsibility* and *advancement* suggest that they form the major strands of high job attitudes. They appear much less frequently in stories of times when the respondents felt unhappy with their job. These motivating factors focussed on the job itself; the 'dissatisfiers' are concerned with the context of environment on the job. Salary has a short-term satisfying effect, but as an influence on job attitudes the research team concluded that it had more potency as a dissatisfier than as a satisfier. In the 'low' stories money tended to reflect a perceived unfairness in the wages policy or system of the company; in the 'high' stories it accompanied achievement: 'it meant more than money; it meant a job well done; it meant that the individual was progressing in his work'.

From their analysis of the 'second-level' factors, Herzberg and his colleagues concluded that:

A sense of personal growth and of self-actualization is the key to an understanding of positive feelings about the job. We would define the first-level factors of *achievement-responsibility-work itself-advancement* as a complex of factors leading to this sense of *personal growth* and *self-actualization*. In a later discussion we postulate a basic need for these goals as a central phenomenon in understanding job attitudes.

Short-term positive feelings can then be regarded as 'partial reinforcements' of these basic needs. The 'satisfiers' of these needs Herzberg named *motivators*. These could be divided into six categories:

MOTIVATORS	
Achievement	Specific successes, such as the successful completion of a job, solutions to problems, vindication, and seeing the results of your work.
Recognition	Any act of recognition, be it notice or praise. A distinction can be made between situations where concrete rewards are given along with the acts of recognition and those in which they are not.
Possibility of Growth	Changes in job situation where the possibilities for professional growth increase. Besides new vistas opened up by promotion they include increased opportunities in the existing situation for learning and practising new skills, or acquiring new professional knowledge.
Advancement	Actual changes which enhance position or status at work.

Responsibility	Being given real responsibility, matched with the necessary authority to discharge it properly.
The Work itself	The actual doing of the job, or phases of it.

Figure 6.2   Factors that Lead to Job Satisfaction

You may have noticed that Herzberg lists *six motivators* above, but only five of them appear in the visual representation (Fig. 6.2). The reason seems to be that Herzberg regarded these five factors as holistically adding up to what he called growth or self-actualization. Personally, I think that was a bit of a mistake, for the category of *possibility of growth* as defined in the chart above is capable of distinction from the other five factors. What do you think?

Herzberg linked the 'hygiene factors' with what he called 'avoidance needs', or the human tendency to avoid painful or unpleasant situations. The *motivators* he now relates directly with the concept that man's 'ultimate goal' is self-actualization or self-realization.

In the work situation this general basic need finds a degree of fulfilment if the job allows some meeting of the related needs for *professional growth* and for the exercise of *creativity*. If these possibilities are intrinsically absent from the job, then heavy compensations in terms of hygiene factors would be necessary to adjust the balance. 'The motivators fit the need for creativity, the hygiene factors satisfy the need for fair treatment, and it is thus that the appropriate incentive must be present to achieve the desired job attitude and job performance.'

HERZBERG AND MASLOW COMPARED

It is interesting to compare Herzberg's theory with Maslow's. They both, you will have spotted, share much the same assumptions about self-actualization. In contrast to the predominantly holistic bias of Maslow's mind, however, Herzberg's approach dichotomizes or divides into two. Now it is possible that the opposite ends or poles of continuums in human behaviour may appear to take on a qualitative difference. By documenting such a phenomenon in relation to work Herzberg indirectly drew attention to what might be the differing characteristics of Maslow's list of conative needs. Physiological, safety and social needs, for example, might create dissatisfaction if they were not met, but – according to Herzberg – they have little power to afford satisfaction. By contrast, the meeting of esteem and self-actualization or professional growth needs could lead to a more positive and longer-lasting sense of satisfaction. In this way we could try to reconcile the two approaches of Maslow and Herzberg.

Incidentally, one of the advantages of Herzberg's two-factor model over Maslow's continuum stems from the tendency of our minds to pick up or perceive contrast. If something can be sharply delineated in black and white, with distinctive contours, our brains register it. This is why teachers so often gravitate naturally towards using dichotomies. (It is the same with movement – if something stays still the brain tends not to perceive it.) Thus Herzberg's dualistic framework has value as a stimulating and introductory visual sketch-map in teaching. But it still becomes an over-simplification if taken beyond a certain point. We can interpret his apparent contradiction of Maslow as more a symptom of differences in casts of mind rather than anything more fundamental in theory.

HERZBERG IN PERSPECTIVE

Herzberg and his colleagues recognized that they were making an inference when arguing from the particular (203 Pittsburg engineers and accountants) to the general, but they felt that the 'lack of individual differences in the occurrence of factors and effects argues the applicability of our findings beyond the immediate bounds of the small sample with which we worked.' They predicted that similar studies of a broader spectrum of educational and occupational backgrounds would reveal wider differences than they had found by comparing engineers with accountants. They expected less 'satisfiers' to be uncovered by research on routine assembly-line workers, for example, but the quality of the unhappy work experiences would probably vary little according to type of job or educational level.

In *Work and the Nature of Man* (1963), Herzberg could report the completion of some seventeen replications of the initial work, using the same research methodology but under the direction of other investigators, which included studies of the following occupations:

- Finnish Supervisors
- Women in the Professions
- Hospital Nurses
- Scientists
- Manufacturing Supervisors
- Female Assemblers
- Unskilled Hospital Employees

- Hungarian Engineers
- Technicians

Herzberg concluded that these studies verified his 'Motivation-Hygiene Theory'. Any discrepancies between them and the Pittsburg findings could be explained away. For example, the fact that *salary* was mentioned only once as a significant dissatisfier and as often as not appeared as a satisfier led to a justification for Herzberg's early view that money belonged primarily to 'hygiene', or the context of the job, along the following lines:

1. Negative effect of salary, when coupled with a dissatisfaction event, endures much longer than the positive results when it is associated with a satisfaction event.
2. Negatively money always reflected discontent with other hygiene factors, and positively it accompanied or marked advancement.
3. All hygiene needs are connected with salary and, because of this, *salary* is the most visible, communicable and advertised factor in all the world of work. *Salary* permeates the thoughts and expressions of people when they view their jobs. In such a circumstance, it is hardly surprising that *salary* often seems to be a satisfier to the individual. If so many hygiene needs can be fulfilled by money, then it is difficult not to conceive of it as a source of happiness.'

Herzberg's treatment of another 'inversion', as he called the phenomenon of a 'motivator' being reported as a 'dissatisfier' and *vice versa*, raises other questions. Three of the seventeen groups studied found positive satisfaction in the *inter-personal relationships* on the job. The first, a group of lower-level supervisors in utility companies, reported that getting along with their subordinates made them more happy than failure to get along with them made them unhappy. Herzberg interpreted this finding in relation to their level of management and the kind of organizations in which they worked as evidence of 'a kind of pathology or sickness in their motivational pattern'. This conclusion I find bizarre. Indeed, Herzberg's general view that 'supervision' (he never called it leadership) is a hygiene factor obstinately ignores the fact that in many circumstances human relationships are as much intrinsic to the job as they are extrinsic. His attempt to distinguish between *inter-personal relationships* and *supervision-technical* does not alter his under-estimation of the satisfying or motivating influence of good leadership.

Herzberg appears to have had a curiously rigid idea about management. The idea that leaders at all levels might be aware and respond to the needs of those working under them does not seem to have occurred to him at all. A stress on the vital importance of good leadership to ensure achievement and recognition, the delegation of responsibility and the provision of challenging tasks, finds no place in his writings, although he did allow that better supervision would be required if jobs were to be made more intrinsically satisfying.

Consider Herzberg's cavalier treatment of the two groups of professional women in government service who found some satisfaction in effective *inter-personal relationships* with their subordinates and fellow employees. In Herzberg's 'rational explanation' these innocent feelings were interpreted as 'a sickness in motivation . . . brought about by the insecurity of women in competing in a traditionally masculine domain.' These comments illustrate the danger that Herzberg's dichotomy between 'satisfaction' and 'dissatisfaction', job content and job context, can become a Procrustean bed upon which all experience, suitably lopped and trimmed, must be made to fit. In fact there is considerable evidence, as we shall see, that leadership and good human relationships contribute to both work achievement and individual job satisfaction.

As you may have guessed, the hypothesis that there are exclusive sets of 'satisfiers' and 'dissatisfiers' has been challenged. Later research has tended to blur the sharp edges of the dichotomy by showing that intrinsic factors may act as dissatisfiers and extrinsic (or contextual) factors can serve as satisfiers.

There is the useful distinction mentioned above between satisfaction *in* a job and satisfaction *with* a job. But those who have attempted an impartial review of the literature in the 'Herzberg controversy' have concluded that the intrinsic-extrinsic dichotomy does not adequately reflect the sources of positive and negative attitudes to work: in short, they regard it as an over-simplification.

On a more positive note, the research work of Herzberg and his colleagues, and the studies which his theory has provoked, did at least confirm the view that work in industry and large organizations can be a means for satisfying a wide range of human needs. It is also an important finding that if work does not provide adequate means of meeting the lower needs, it is experienced as positively dissatisfying, more so if opportunities for more intrinsic satisfactions are also missing.

With his shock of grey hair and fund of good stories, backed by research and illustrated by videos, Herzberg himself was a prophetic figure on public platforms throughout the world. His seminars, as I have already recalled, were charged with almost evangelical fervour for the gospel that industrial work, as much as any other form of work, should serve the humanistic purpose of self-actualization. So much so that jobs which do not lend themselves to this end are to be *enriched* until they do, or automated out of existence.

> If the building of a bridge does not enrich the awareness of those who work on it, then that bridge ought not to be built.
> Franz Fanon in *The Wretched of the Earth* (1961)

In cases where mechanization or automation is impossible, 'hygiene factors', such as big financial rewards, must clearly be seen to be compensations for being sub-human. But with such a new faith in man and some professional ingenuity, it will be possible to enrich most jobs so that they win more of both intrinsic satisfactions and extrinsic rewards for the worker.

In terms of the three-circles model (see p. 91), Herzberg clearly stressed factors in the *task* circle – achievement, recognition, responsibility, the work itself, possibilities of growth – as being central to motivation and high job satisfaction. But he undervalued the *team* circle, not seeing the group or organization as a potential – and often actual – source of both satisfaction and motivation. He completely missed the mark in his estimation of managers and supervisors. One British research project, for example, showed conclusively that shop floor workers in the study perceived their supervisors as being sources of both support and motivation. Incidentally, it also made the point that whereas 70 per cent of satisfied workers found their jobs more interesting, varied, challenging and allowing more opportunities for achievement and the use of their abilities, the other 30 per cent in the *same* job were dissatisfied. Clearly individual attitudes and values inevitably produce different perceptions of the same job!

Paradoxically, although Herzberg had nothing to say about the importance of leadership in management, the implementation of his programme for reforming or enriching jobs in industry depended entirely upon it. Fortunately his advent corresponded with a growing sense that more leadership – at all levels including the top – was needed if innovation and change were to become the order of the day. As Pehr Gyllenhammar, then President of Volvo in Sweden, said,

Leadership is having the courage to put a stake on an idea, and risk making mistakes. Leadership is being able to draw new boundaries, beyond the existing limits of ideas and activities. Only through this kind of leadership can we keep our institutions from drifting aimlessly, to no purpose.

And he also practised what he preached; as you will see from the case study below.

CASE STUDY: VOLVO LEADS THE WAY

One of the earliest experiments in enriching work happened at Volvo, the Swedish car manufacturers. In 1968 labour turnover at Torslanda, Volvo's traditional factory, was 52 per cent. The 'average' worker thus felt the need to change jobs every two years. 'To me,' says the company's president, Pehr Gyllenhammar, 'this seems horrifying.' Eliminating the root cause of boredom, he concludes, asks for a completely new approach to production and organization, so that 'work' must be adapted to people, not people to machines. A chance to put this philosophy into practice came with the building of a new factory at Kalmar. A revolutionary design established 500 production people into 25 groups, each group expert on a subassembly electrical system, or instrumentation, or interiors. The team organizes its own work methods, is responsible for its own inspection and controls its own work pace. Work is brought to the team by computer controlled carriers. These can also be controlled manually by the team.

Kalmar acted as a catalyst for other plants including the 8,000 strong Torslanda factory. The pattern of gradual evolution established there repeated itself at other plants.

'It sometimes scares me that what we do in Volvo is presented to others as an innovation,' said Gyllenhammar, 'because this demonstrates, after all, how little has been done in work organization. Companies spend almost endless hours trying to provide change, incentive, interest, involvement, and motivation for top executives, yet almost no time is spent in looking at the rest of the work force in the same way. Until now, managers have not found it necessary. We are still in the era that Adam Smith described so many years ago, where "a worker gives up his ease, his liberty and his happiness when he goes into industry".

'If we can give the worker back his ease, his liberty and his happiness, or at least provide conditions under which he can find them for himself, I believe we will come closer to a healthy, human "post-industrial" society.'

Few strategic business leaders, however, had the vision and enthusiasm of the Volvo chief. Most American and European companies preferred to wait and follow, rather than give a lead. As one managing director said to me at the time, 'Change? We don't want that — things are bad enough already.'

CONCLUSION

Longer-lasting or deeper satisfaction at work goes hand-in-hand with the factors that Herzberg labelled the 'motivators': achievement, recognition, work itself, responsibility, and advancement. Together for him these added up to the 'growth' dimension of a job — its self-actualizing properties.

In making such a sharp dichotomy between hygiene and motivators Herzberg revealed what has been called a 'two-value orientation'. Such black-and-white thinking can aid intellectual digestion, but it can also lead to oversimplification. Money could not be fitted into this Procrustean bed without some mutilation. Its role in motivation will receive a fuller exploration elsewhere in this book. Even so, there is some evidence — as we have seen — that, for many people at least, money can soon lose its motivating power if you have enough of it. Equally, it can make you very dissatisfied if you feel that you are being unfairly or inadequately rewarded for your work.

Yet Herzberg's motivators provide you with a useful checklist for assessing each role or job in your organization. These motivators are some of the main nutrients or vitamins needed in fulfilling work. As a manager you should consider enriching jobs or empowering people so that the possibility of these longer-lasting satisfactions is really there. All the seven strategies for you to consider in Part Three reflect the importance of the 'motivators'. By putting them into practice you will help to infuse a vocational spirit into those who work as partners with you. Not before time, too. For as the famous potter Bernard Leach once said: 'You cannot starve people too long of a heartbeat in work.'

PART TWO

BRIDGING THE GAP

The general philosophy and theoretical framework behind
understanding motivation, which we explored in PART
ONE, can easily lie stagnant in one pigeon-hole in your
mind, or remain stored in the business books on your shelf
without being put to use. Your daily practice, even by
those who know all the theory, can remain a matter of
applying the 'stick-and-carrot' approach.

Part Two is like a railway junction where the various
lines in the first six chapters converge into your SELF-
CONCEPT as a manager. Transmuted in this way they
become ACTIONABLE along the lines that leave this
junction and thread their way through Part Three.

By the time you have completed this part you should have:

1. understood motivational theories and research in the
   context of the THREE-CIRCLES MODEL of your core
   responsibilities as a manager.

2. formed a clear idea of the role of LEADERSHIP in the
   management of people, especially in the domain of
   motivation.

3. deepened your own commitment to develop to the full
   your SKILLS as a leader-manager.

7

THE THREE-CIRCLES MODEL

Having explored the various theories and research on motivation that have some claim to our attention, we need to pull the threads together. How can we best understand these theories?

The three-circles model, I suggest, provides us with the best framework available for seeing individual needs, motives and values in perspective. In the next two chapters I shall use them as a means of summarizing the story so far. Then I shall develop them as a springboard for Part Three – the seven practical strategies both you and your organization can apply in order to draw the best from the people who work for you.

THE OVERLAPPING AREAS OF NEED

In *Effective Leadership* (1989) I suggested that there are in fact *three* areas of overlapping needs present in working groups or organizations: the need to accomplish the common task, the needs of the group or team for unity and the needs which individuals bring with them by virtue of being both human and personal. The circles are dynamic in the sense that each of them possesses its own motivational forces in a magnetic field. These fields interact positively or negatively.

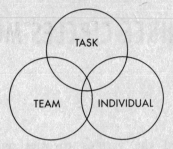

Figure 7.1   The Trefoil Model of Needs

The circles or areas of need will affect each other if there is a *positive* change in any one of them. For example:

- Achievement in terms of a common aim tends to build a sense of group identity – the 'we-feeling', as some have called it. The moment of victory closes the psychological gaps between people: morale rises naturally.
- Good internal communications and a developed team spirit based upon past successes make a group much more likely to do well in its task area, and incidentally provide a more satisfactory climate for the individual.
- An individual whose needs are recognized and who feels that he or she can make a characteristic and worthwhile contribution both to the task and the group will tend to produce good fruits in both these areas.

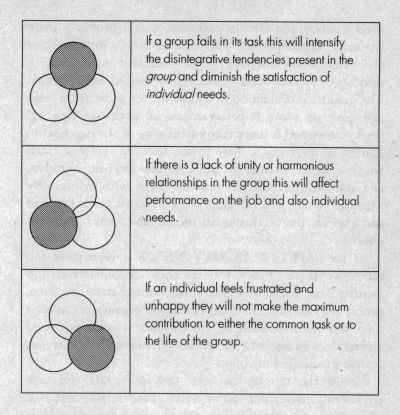

	If a group fails in its task this will intensify the disintegrative tendencies present in the *group* and diminish the satisfaction of *individual* needs.
	If there is a lack of unity or harmonious relationships in the group this will affect performance on the job and also individual needs.
	If an individual feels frustrated and unhappy they will not make the maximum contribution to either the common task or to the life of the group.

Figure 7.2 Interaction of Needs

In the context of the general theory of the three circles you can see above how the meeting of individual needs is dependent upon the two other areas. Take Maslow's PHYSIOLOGICAL NEEDS – your own and your family's – as a starter. Work groups and teams are linear descendants of the hunting and gathering bands of our remote forefathers. After the hunt the food was exchanged and shared out, doubtless according to traditional formulas. The male hunters and female gatherers would probably share the meat, vegetables and fruit in their family groups. Later the practice of bartering – the beginnings of trade – developed so that food could be exchanged for artefacts. The gradual introduction of coined money some 3000 years ago gave us a much better means of exchange than its predecessors and a more convenient way of storing wealth. Instead of receiving a share in the hunting spoils or catch we now receive money in order to buy food for ourselves and our families and to provide them with houses. By working we are still meeting our individual needs for food and shelter, but – thanks to money and banks – at one remove.

As for SAFETY/SECURITY NEEDS, a permanent job can allay these. Pension is another critical factor. Job security and financial security are wanted more by some people than others. These days far fewer employers can offer total job security, such as, for instance, I once possessed several decades ago when I was an 'established' civil servant – a job guaranteed for life.

Notice the tension between the individual and task circles in this respect. Some tasks involve risk, and risk often threatens the safety/security needs of the individuals concerned at the most fundamental level. In the fishing industry, for example, in which I once worked myself, there is still a relatively high death rate from the loss of trawlers and accidents at sea.

But our need for food for ourselves and our children, and our need for security, fundamental though these needs are, does not exhaust the concept of individual needs. We have SOCIAL NEEDS as well. As we have already seen, organizations such as companies, regiments, universities, schools or churches all play a large part in meeting our social needs. Both men and women miss the camaraderie of work when for one reason or another, they can no longer go to work.

Working together on a common task provides opportunities for achievement, both corporate and individual. Achievement builds self-confidence and attracts recognition from others, thereby meeting your ESTEEM NEEDS. Your self-esteem, of course, doesn't come solely from the tasks or the teams to which you contribute. But, past or present, they play a major role. Witness the fact that the state can give unemployed people money to pay for food and shelter, and it can give them a measure of financial security, but there is no handout for self-respect or the respect of others: that comes from working together on a common task. Consequently self-esteem is the first casualty of permanent unemployment.

There remains Maslow's need for self-actualization. You may recall that he believed a common external task was essential if that need is to be met.

THE STEEP AND STONY PATH TO SELF-ACTUALIZATION

This business of self-actualization via a commitment to an important job and to worthwhile work could also be said, then, to be the path to human happiness (by contrast with the direct attack or the direct search for happiness – happiness is an epiphenomenon, a by-product, something not to be sought directly but an indirect reward for virtue). The other way – of seeking for personal salvation – just doesn't work for anybody I have *ever* seen – that is the introspection, the full-time-in-a-cave all by one's self some place. This may work for people in India and Japan – I won't deny that – but I have never seen it work for anybody in all my

> ## THE STEEP AND STONY PATH TO SELF-ACTUALIZATION (Cont)
>
> experience in the United States. The only happy people I know are the ones who are working well at something they consider important. Also, I have pointed out in my lecture and in my previous writings that this was universal truth for all my self-actualizing subjects . . . expressed in their devotion to, dedication to, and identification with some great and important job. This was true for every single case.
>
> Or I can put this very bluntly: *Salvation is a By-Product of Self-Actualizing Work and Self-Actualizing Duty.*
>
> Abraham Maslow, *Eupsychian Management:*
> *A Journal* (1965)

What is interesting is that some recent research confirms that people do *need*, even if they do not always *like*, the *demanding* element in tasks. But before describing that research, it is worth exploring briefly the concept of task.

THE NATURE OF TASK

Deriving from the same root as *tax*, our work *task* originally meant a tax or service imposed by a fuedal superior, and hence a piece of work imposed, exacted or undertaken as a duty or the like. So the word carries overtones of something hard or unpleasant. A task needs to be done. The word suggests an undertaking that will require a relative amount of effort.

THE TASK IS GIVEN

Next you should note what might be called the *givenness* implied by task. A task is usually assigned or imposed by some superior, such as a teacher or employer. Alternatively, the tasker or taskmaster may not be a person as such but the circumstances or situation in which you find yourself. If you are one of a party of people who are shipwrecked on a Pacific island or who have crashlanded in the jungles of South America, then the novel circumstances will force upon you a set of tasks. Shelters have to be built, food and water gathered, the sick or injured cared for and a rescue operation planned.

The point about a task is that it exists, so to speak, outside the group or the individual: it is something there that needs to be done. It is a given, either by a lawful authority or by circumstances. There isn't much choice. Natural tasks are those which living as humans in our natural environment imposes upon us, such as our need to eat. The basic task of all humans is to find enough food in order to stay alive, hence the hunting and gathering activities of prehistoric men and women were essentially task activities. We have no choice but to eat.

That doesn't mean to say that a group cannot come together and identify or choose their own task. I know a small group of four or five businessmen who set themselves a demanding trek in some relatively inaccessible part of the world each year. Because we enjoy task-centred activity together, at least in retrospect, we create other occasions for it in sport and leisure.

ALL WORK AND NO PLAY

Work today has lost many traditional characteristics; so has play. Play has increasingly been transformed into organized sports, and sports, in turn, increasingly resemble work in the hard practice and preparation, in the intense involvement of coaches and athletes (in the spirit of work), and in actual economic productivity.

In a final paradox, only those sports which began as work – that is, hunting and fishing – are now dominated by the spirit of play.

John Talamini and Charles Page, *Sport and Society*

We set ourselves mountains – actual or metaphorical – to climb. But even here there is a sense of imposition: the task is there, outside ourselves, as a challenge, and once we accept it we are under a sense of duty or obligation to see it through, despite its hardships, sufferings and penalties. Why else do mountaineers endure the loss of their fingers or toes through frostbite?

WHAT IS IT ABOUT JOBS THAT GIVE PEOPLE MOST SATISFACTION?

There is nothing like work to keep you satisfied, a British Psychological Society conference was told. Unemployed people often try to obtain the same sense of satisfaction by working hard at their leisure but without complete success, said Dr John Haworth of Manchester University.

The trouble with leisure, he found, was that there was no supervisor forcing you to do things you would rather avoid. Overcoming a reluctance to carry out tasks that were unpleasant led to much satisfaction.

Apart from the financial rewards, work promotes happiness by providing workers with a time-structure, social contacts, a collective purpose, a sense of identity and more regular activity.

Research among young unemployed people has shown that these benefits can be obtained outside work, usually by more work-like and active leisure pursuits, and that those who take part in them are generally happier and feel more positive about themselves. However, the rewards still fall short of real work.

The difference is motivation. At work, there is little choice but to persist with tasks that would otherwise have been given up, and this ultimately produces a sense of satisfaction and well-being. Leisure, which is self-motivated, is seldom able to produce the same results.

Among managers, a sense of collective purpose and status are the most important routes to high self-esteem. During leisure time, active pursuits are most often linked to being satisfied with life.

Dr Haworth concludes that much of the frustration resulting from unemployment can be mitigated, but many things about work are difficult to mimic.

The research reported above has real political and social significance, apart from providing some confirmation of the three-circles model. These findings are so important that it's worth including here the perceptive commentary upon them by the leader-writer of *The Times* (the italics are mine).

'What it suggests is that the kind of self-esteem and satisfaction that most people feel to be necessary for a fulfilled life can rarely be achieved outside paid work. In other words, no matter how worthwhile or energetic a leisure pastime may be, it cannot impart the same sense of purpose and self-respect as a "proper" job.

The research paper, by Dr John Haworth of Manchester University, does not simply equate this unique kind of satisfaction with the fact of being paid. There seems to be a more subtle psychological difference between working for a livelihood and even the most assiduous hobby. What is suggested by the responses of those who filled in Dr Haworth's questionnaires is that *the very constraints of working life are what make it satisfying.* The findings refer to factors like "time structure, social contact, collective purpose, social identity or status, and regular activity." In plain English, these amount to having to be at a given place at a particular time with actual deadlines for completed tasks, working toward some larger goal with a team of people in which everyone has a specified role and having all of this take place in some customary, habitual way.

Being compelled to take part by some force outside personal whim – what Dr Haworth calls "extrinsic motivation" as opposed to "intrinsic" – seems to be the key factor in making paid work a more valuable source of psychological well-being. Having objectives and structures imposed by others lends credibility to an enterprise. In leisure activities – even ones that are socially useful – the freedom to create personal goals and time limits often degenerates into an open-ended activity in which people find it difficult to maintain a sense of purpose.

People specifically mentioned that being at work *often involved doing things which were initially disliked. The overcoming of their own resistance to complete the task gave a form of gratification that was peculiarly difficult to match outside the workplace.'*

You will notice that what we need is not always the same as what we want. Helping people over the stile of their initial dislike for what has to be done – especially if it involves change – clearly calls for leadership. The donkey in us doesn't always like being entered for a steeplechase. But the donkey is capable of growing wings. It can even soar like Pegasus, given the right leadership.

> Ah, but a man's reach should exceed his grasp.
> Or what's a heaven for?
>
> *Robert Browning*

CONCLUSION

There are three overlapping areas of need at work, each with its motivational field. They can be compared to the three overlapping areas of red, green and blue into which light refracts. Just as a television picture is made up of dots and these three primary additive colours (and the three secondary colours where they overlap), so daily life at work is composed of complex interactions of task, team and individual. But it's only when you stand back that you see the three circles take shape.

The elements of difficulty and demand in the task, the 'otherness' or 'givenness' in it, are coherent with human nature. Providing, of course, the task in question has value. Tasks that you are forced to do and that lack any personal meaning fall into the category of toil or drudgery. The ultimate symbol of them is the treadmill.

The three-circles model gives us a most useful sketchmap

available of the core responsibility of a leader. In this chapter it has also helped us:

- to understand the contributions of motivational theorists;
- to place them in perspective;
- to put them to work.

8

BALANCING THE BALLOONS

Imagine now that the three circles TASK, TEAM and INDIVIDUAL are three large coloured balloons. You have a cylinder with a limited supply of gas. You can either inflate the balloons equally or you can put more gas into one at the expense of the other. The latter course, if it's your conscious or unconscious decision to do so, will result in some distortion of the model.

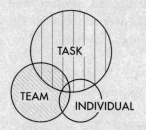

Here the TASK is blown up hard and the PEOPLE circles have shrunk. Frederick Taylor's emphasis in 'scientific management' on productivity at the expense of team work and the individual fits this pattern.

Although the TASK does have a priority in work situations, and should always be the top circle, it can be overemphasized. As a leader you should be task-focused, but not blind to the other circles.

EXERCISE

You are skipper of a company-sponsored yacht in a round-the-world race. Your sponsor badly needs some good publicity. One day to go and you are rapidly overhauling the front-runner, a Japanese trimaran. Suddenly one of the crew goes overboard in rough weather. To stop now will cost you the race. What would you do?

In the above distorted model of the three circles the individual is subordinate to the task, a mere means to an end. Higher wages are used to compensate or reward such self-subordination. A cost may be paid in physical and mental health.

Owners and managers have a natural bias towards this state of affairs. For many corporations are driven by the profit motive. That is mainly why trade unions and professional associations came into being: to protect and promote the interests of the individual over and against the interests of the task and the group or organization.

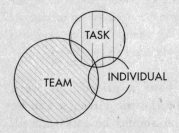

The TEAM or ORGANIZATION balloon is now over-inflated at some expense to the TASK but at more to the INDIVIDUAL. The 'Human Relations' school, linked to Elton Mayo and the Hawthorne experiments, ties in with this model.

This over-emphasis on the value of the group and the paramount need to belong may reflect a phase in most people's personal development. It can also characterize certain cultures, as it did in America during the post-Second World War period. It is still a marked feature in Japanese society, where individuals tend to be culturally conditioned to put the group or organization first.

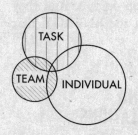

The blown-up INDIVIDUAL balloon has reduced the values of TASK and TEAM. They are seen to be secondary in importance to the needs of the INDIVIDUAL, including self-actualization. Maslow's and Herzberg's philosophies fall roughly into this camp.

You can now see clearly that Maslow and Herzberg's theories can be interpreted or understood partly as overreactions against the over-inflations of the TASK and TEAM balloons. As such they played a necessary part. By filling in the sketchmap of individual needs and motivation they made it possible for us to adjust the valves on the cylinder and reach a more balanced model.

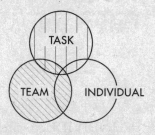

The fact that the three circles are now shown in equal sizes doesn't mean, of course, that they should all receive equal attention at all times from you as a leader. You may well have to be extremely task-centred for a sustained period. Even then – if you are a good leader – you will find or create time to strengthen your team and encourage each individual member of it, for they will probably be working as hard as you are. But you do have to invest in those two PEOPLE circles at other times. If you don't, those two wells (to change metaphors) will dry up on you. And they are your oil wells – the sources of all the ENERGY that you have at your disposal.

TRANSACTIONAL AND TRANSFORMATIONAL RELATIONS

How does 'expectancy theory' tie into the three-circles model? If you transpose the model to the corporate level then it looks like this:

Figure 8.1   Three Core Areas

You will see that the INDIVIDUAL circle has remained unchanged. When you join an organization there will always be a legal contract which lists what is expected of you and what you may legitimately expect of the ORGAN-IZATION, including:

- your duties or contribution to the corporate work (job description)
- how you relate to the whole (your place in the structure)
- the financial reward for your services.

The latter is fairly crucial, because money is our principal means of exchange; it is thus the way in which many of the needs listed by Maslow – encompassing your family's individual needs as well as your own – will be met.

In fact, as we have seen, many more nonfinancial or nonmaterial needs or motives will find at least partial fulfilment in the context of shared human enterprise. Let me recapitulate the ways in which the TASK and TEAM dimensions meet Maslow's five sets of needs.

INDIVIDUAL NEED	TASK/TEAM
Physiological	Work on the TASK provides money, which pays the supermarket food bills and the mortgage for you and your family.
Safety/Security	Again money contributes by paying for insurance and pensions. In terms of your physical security the TEAM can be vital. An airline pilot trusts the engineer to screw on the petrol caps.

INDIVIDUAL NEED	TASK/TEAM (Cont)
Social	The TEAM at work – or rather the network of teams, such as project groups and the ORGANIZATION itself is vital here. Add in the relationships with long-term suppliers and customers or clients.
Esteem	You can give an unemployed person money for food and shelter, but it's not easy to give them the respect of others or self-respect if it's wanting. For they are bound up with being a valued member of a TEAM in pursuit of a common TASK.
Self-Actualization (in the particular sense)	Self-actualization is a by-product of commitment and hard work on an important TASK that you feel personally drawn to do – to the very limits of your ability. There are no other easier routes or short-cuts.

Figure 8.2   Individual Needs in Relation to Task and Team

In concluding the mutual contract you make with the organization you will be calculating, and perhaps negotiating, along the lines of expectancy theory. Is this job worth the effort? How good is the salary? What are my expectations? What are their expectations?

Both the organization and yourself will be assessing the degree of overlapping common interest between you both. The organization will want to know that both opportunity and financial rewards are sufficient to motivate you. For your part you will no doubt be asking the same question.

But this kind of rational calculation, backed ultimately by a legal contract, is only the beginning of the story. There is a considerable difference between the legal minimum that a contract requires each party to give to the other and the potential that each has to do the other good in the context of the shared common purpose.

In Part Three I shall be describing six ways to secure the best from people, as opposed to the legal minimum or even an above-average level of energy and commitment. But, with the laws of reciprocity and equivalent exchange in mind, let me say now that you will never get the best unless you are the best and give the best. Those organizations who want to travel this road are not facing an easy journey. It demands, for instance, the transformation of managers into leaders. Leaders give themselves, and that will often – not always – win a response in kind.

Usually it's only unique situations – such as a great crisis – which evoke that true glory of human nature. But it is there. There are plenty of instances when individuals transcend themselves in the service of some cause or love that they sense is great. This magnanimity or greatness of spirit both looks for good leadership and responds to it when it is there. A psychological contract of trust and mutual self-giving can develop between leaders and their colleagues which is immensely strong. It has to be two-way, although this is often with generous attitudes and actions on the part of the leader.

DOCTOR JOHNSON ON THE BRITISH SOLDIER

Dr Samuel Johnson, scholar and author of the first English dictionary, once remarked that the special characteristic of the British soldier is a species of magnanimity. 'His greatness of heart is exhibited not only in bravery,' Johnson continued, 'but in the qualities he expects in his officers. He relies on them to lead him, and the officers on their part are quite satisfied the soldiers will follow them.'

'Do the soldiers then lack initiative?' he was asked. 'Not at all,' Johnson replied. 'Each red-coated soldier considers his officer's leadership a tribute to his own loyalty and *esprit de corps*. In the case of other nations,' he added, 'the officers do not lead their men, but follow behind to ensure that there is no skulking to the rear.'

The building of such a psychological contract, based on mutual trust, lies at the heart of management. It is the challenge facing your organizations today if they truly aspire to excellence.

CONCLUSION

In summary here are some tentative principles about human nature which may serve as a bridge between the two parts — practical and theoretical — of this book. To be both realistic and visionary about people is not a common gift but it is part of your calling as a leader. Paradoxical, unpredictable, mysterious as they are, people will reveal this greatness to those who recognize them for what they can be.

- We are individual persons but we only become fully persons and truly ourselves in relation to other persons and meaningful work.
- We are creative and imaginative, but only in concert with others – whether we work on our own or in a team.
- We do like to achieve, but our individual achievements only prove to be really effective as part of a team.
- We are self-motivated and self-directed, but we still look for leadership within our field, if only to coordinate our activities with others and to remind us occasionally of who we are.
- We are intelligent enough to know the difference between extrinsic rewards – such as money – and the less tangible but very real intrinsic rewards of work; both are important to us in different degrees, according to our own individual value systems.
- We have a latent desire to leave the world a better place than when we found it, and if our work can contribute to that end – even at a cost to ourselves – it yields us an inestimable bonus.

No description of human nature can ever be complete, but you only have to be 90 per cent right about 90 per cent of the people with whom you are dealing. Of course there will be bad days. Of course there will be exceptions. But people respond to those who have vision. That vision should include a realistic but uplifting view of people, such as the one I have sketched above.

> *If you treat people as they are, they will stay as they are. But if you treat them as they ought to be, they will become bigger and better persons.*
>
> *Goethe*

9

LEADERSHIP AND MOTIVATION

As appointed leader you have responsibility for meeting the three overlapping areas of need. That doesn't mean to say that you do all the work yourself – too much is required for any one person to do it all. But you are the conductor of the orchestra, all of whose members should be contributing in each of the areas.

Figure 9.1   Core Responsibilities of Leadership

LEADERSHIP FUNCTIONS

Clearly, in order that the group should fulfil its task and be held together as a working team, certain *functions* will have to be performed. By function in this context I mean any behaviour, words or actions which meet one or more spheres of the needs, or *areas of leadership responsibility* as they may also be called. Defining the aim, planning, and encouraging the group, are examples of what is meant by a function. See below for a fuller list.

FUNCTION	ELEMENTS
Planning	Seeking all available information Defining group task, purpose or goal Making a workable plan (in right decision-making framework)
Initiating	Briefing group on the aims and the plan Explaining *why* aim or plan is necesssary Allocating tasks to group members Setting group standards
Controlling	Maintaining group standards Influencing tempo Ensuring all actions are taken towards objectives Keeping discussion relevant Prodding group to action/decision
Supporting	Expressing acceptance of persons and their contribution Encouraging group/individuals Disciplining group/individuals Creating team spirit Relieving tension with humour Reconciling disagreements or getting others to explore them

FUNCTION	ELEMENTS (Cont)
Informing	Clarifying task and plan Giving new information to the group, i.e. keeping them 'in the picture' Receiving information from group Summarizing suggestions and ideas coherently
Evaluating	Checking feasibility of an idea Testing the consequences of a proposed solution Evaluating group performance Helping the group to evaluate its own performance against standards

Figure 9.2 Some Key Leadership Functions

The names and the definitions of functions are by no means fixed. But the essential activities of *defining the task, planning, briefing, controlling, supporting* (the team and individual circles), *informing* (the linking role of leadership), and *evaluating* are all clearly responsible and tend to recur on most lists.

'Should not *motivating* be among them?' I was asked at one seminar. Before I could reply, my questioner answered his own question. 'But perhaps motivation is the result of performing all the functions well.'

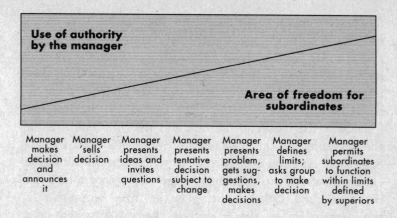

Use of authority by the manager						Area of freedom for subordinates
Manager makes decision and announces it	Manager 'sells' decision	Manager presents ideas and invites questions	Manager presents tentative decision subject to change	Manager presents problem, gets suggestions, makes decisions	Manager defines limits; asks group to make decision	Manager permits subordinates to function within limits defined by superiors

Figure 9.3   A Continuum of Shared Decisions

SHARING DECISIONS

Without forgetting the broader opportunities open to members for supplementing the work of leadership in all three areas described above it is especially useful to examine specifically the extent to which the leader should share with others the general function of *decision-making*, the core of such more definite functions as setting objectives and planning.

In an invaluable diagram in the *Harvard Business Review* (1959) Tannenbaum and Schmidt plotted the possibilities of participation. The diagram can be compared to a cake: at one end the manager has virtually all of it, and at the other the group has the lion's share. In terms of a transaction between a leader and an individual follower the continuum also illustrates the degrees of delegation that are possible in the context of a given decision.

There is much to be said (and that has been said) for moving as far to the right of the continuum as possible, for *the more that people share in decisions which directly affect them the more they are motivated to carry them out* — providing they trust the integrity of the leader who is inviting them to participate in the decision. Yet factors in the *situation* (especially the nature of the task and the time available for the decision) and the *group* (especially the attitudes, knowledge, and experience of members) will naturally limit the extent to which the right-hand edge of the continuum can be approached. Other limiting factors may be present in the personality of the leader or the value system and philosophy of a particular organization, factors which cannot be described as natural or intrinsic in the same way as the situational or group constraints.

There are some groups and organizations whose *characteristic* working situations (as contrasted to the actual ones they may be in for 90 per cent of their time) are essentially crisis ones, where by definition time is short for decisions and the matter of life or death rests upon prompt decisions from one man e.g. operating theatre teams, fire brigades, police forces, air line crews, and military organizations. Yet such groups are not always in crisis situations, and for training purposes, if for no other reasons, they need to explore the decision-making scale. Moreover, although it is not always possible to share decisions over *ends* (i.e. goals, objectives, aims or purpose) it is usually possible to involve others more or less fully in *means* (i.e. methods, techniques, conditions, and plans).

Rather than engaging in the fruitless attempt to establish a particular spot or 'style' on the scale which is 'best' we should see the continuum as a sliding scale, or as a thermometer marked with boiling and freezing points.

Where the latter points fall on the scale will depend upon the characteristic working situation of the group or organization. There will be a difference, for example, between a squad of new recruits in the army and a research group in an electronics or chemical firm.

Why does a person become a leader? The general idea or integrated concept of a leader that emerges from my work is that of a person with:

- certain *qualities* of personality and character which are
- appropriate to the general *situation* and
- supported by a degree of relevant technical knowledge and experience, who is
- able to provide the necessary *functions* to guide a group towards the further realization of its purpose, while
- maintaining and building its unity as a team;
- doing all this in the right ratio or proportion with the contributions of other members of the team.

These points form a framework for drawing together the major strands of research into the nature of leadership without exhausting the inherent mystery present in it as in all human relations.

LEADER OR MANAGER – OR BOTH?

As we have seen, Douglas McGregor suggested in *The Human Side of Enterprise* that organizations and managers could be divided into those that held a low view of man (Theory X) and those who held a high view (Theory Y). Those who hold a high concept of man, as McGregor did, do tend to see management as synonymous with leadership. The experience of the Second World War, and the influence of such powerful advocates of leadership in management as Lord Slim, further encouraged those who adopted what could be called the leadership interpretation of management.

ON THE DIFFERENCE BETWEEN LEADERS AND MANAGERS

'To begin with, we do not talk in the Army of "management" but of "leadership". This is significant. There is a difference between leaders and management. The leader and the men who follow him represent one of the oldest, most natural and most effective of all human relationships. The manager and those he manages are a later product, with neither so romantic nor so inspiring a history.

'Leadership is of the spirit, compounded of personality and vision: its practice is an art. Management is of the mind, more a matter of accurate calculation of statistics, of methods, time tables, and routine: its practice is a science. Managers are necessary; leaders are essential. A good system will produce efficient managers but more than that is needed.

'We must find managers who are not only skilled organizers but inspired and inspiring leaders, destined eventually to fill the highest ranks of control and direction. Such men will gather round them close-knit teams of subordinates like themselves and of technical experts, whose efficiency, enthusiasm and loyalty will be unbeatable. Increasingly this is recognized and the search for leadership is on . . .'

Field Marshal Lord Slim, in an address to the Australian Institute of Management (1957), while he was Governor-General of Australia.

The fragments of a different concept of management still persist. In order to understand it one must remember that managers and under-managers in the nineteenth century were selected largely from the ranks of the professional classes already employed by the entrepreneur-owners; principally they were drawn from engineers and accountants. Now engineers were seen – perhaps unfairly – to be concerned with machines; accountants with figures. Both were systems-minded.

This reliance upon systems (and ultimately upon a more scientific approach), stemming from the dominance of engineers and accountants in the early days of running industrial organizations, gives the concept of management today one of its most important nuances – one that is absent from the concept of leadership. But, as each generation discovers for itself, systems are only half the solution: the other half are the people involved in working the system.

Those early managers and their successors transferred their mechanistic assumptions to the problem of managing 'hands'. They saw humans as things, cogs in a system. The organization as a whole was a machine which they, the managers, were 'running'. This mechanistic philosophy of 'scientific management' is forever associated with the American engineer Frederick W. Taylor, whose influence was most potent between 1905 and 1917.

Setting aside Taylor's view of man, his work does mark a stage in the development of the management concept. The functions of *planning* and *controlling* were heavily emphasized in his work. Above all the introduction of systems and systematic thinking – the application of science to management – held out the promise of increasing productivity.

The concept of management has acquired some definite undertones or connotations over the two or three centuries of its existence, largely from its formative years in the last century, nuances which cling to it like a comet's tail. Some of these are now widely thought to be questionable, such as the mechanistic doctrines of human nature and organization.

On a more positive note, a strong overtone of *administration*, especially financial administration, still remains implicitly or explicitly related to *management*. I think that being a good manager implies that you are a good administrator.

Leadership also has some distinctive overtones. To begin with *change* and *leadership* are two closely related concepts. Change tends to highlight the need for leadership; conversely leaders are likely to create change even where others do not see the need for it. Managers are sometimes seen as being there to achieve the objectives set by others (owners, directors). Leaders are seen to be responsible for new objectives and aims, against a background of thinking through the interplay of the fundamental purpose of the organization and its changing, challenging environment.

Other significant nuances of leadership have been discovered – or rediscovered – in the last ten years. Managers often motivate by balancing rewards and threats; their ways of motivating others may even border on the manipulative. Leaders also reward and punish on occasions, but they also lead by example; they *inspire* confidence and they generate in others a genuine enthusiasm and commitment for the work in hand. 'You can be appointed a manager,' it has been said, 'but you are not a leader until your appointment is ratified in the hearts and minds of those who work for you.'

The relation between managing and leading, then, is an overlapping one. Neither concept must push the other out of existence. Managing at its best is much the same as leading as understood in the functional approach. A manager is often – but not always – a leader in industry or commerce. Like all leaders he or she is also a colleague and subordinate; the team membership role is equally necessary and positive.

No leadership exists in the raw: it is always incarnated in a situation. A business leader needs technical and financial knowledge: he or she must also exemplify the qualities required by those who work in that field. A leader of managers should personify the qualities of a good manager. These include the distinctive management virtue of being a good administrator of such resources as money, property and time. A manager will also respect and use systems, for the balance between order and freedom is the essence of organization.

Leadership has certain overtones – a sense of direction, vision and inspiration – which are now relevant in management at all levels. Leadership is defined by those three areas of need:

- achieving the task
- building and maintaining the team
- motivating and developing the individual.

As such it is now your core responsibility as a business leader or manager. Notice that motivating others is now centre-stage in your managerial role.

TAKING THE HELIVIEW

One big difference between leaders and managers is that leaders are much more visible. Then you can stimulate, prod, encourage and even inspire as the situation requires. And be there when you are needed.

Therefore, as a leader you should be simultaneously detached and ready to intervene where and when necessary. By detached I don't mean remote or absent. Indeed, as I have just said, it is essential that you stay in close touch. That's the real reason why you should either get out of your office, or – better still – not have an office in the old sense at all.

Why do you need to 'walk the job' or meet those who are actually doing it? The worst reasons are to do it for the sake of appearances – as a kind of personal public relations exercise – or because you have bought the latest management fashion. MBWA (Management by Walking About) is one of those bright ideas. A senior manager who lacks real purpose walking around the factory can be both ineffective and counterproductive.

Arthur Henderson, the chief executive of Rollerbearings, a major engineering company, had worked his way to the top by way of becoming the finance director. An accountant by profession, he believed that a business could be run by budgets. His new Director of Human Resources, however, persuaded him that he should practise MBWA.

People in the office at first seem pleased to see him. He chatted about his golf game last Saturday and then told them about his decision to move them all into an open-plan office next year, at which they seemed rather unhappy. On the shopfloor he talked about the local football team to one or two lathe-workers, and then stopped another forklift driver, who seemed in a bit of a hurry, for a few words. 'Any questions?' he asked at the end of the conversation. 'Yes,' replied the driver, 'who the hell are you?'

A group of senior business leaders concluded a week's visit to Japanese carmaker Toyota's main plant by meeting the President of the company. 'Could you tell us,' asked one of them, 'why you spend so much time out of your office? In our country we have so much paperwork to do that we cannot get out and about like you do.'

'Ladies and gentlemen,' replied the President of Toyota, 'it's very simple. We do not make Toyota cars in my office.'

Toyota's corporate leader is nearer to the mark than Arthur Henderson in the story. As a leader you should

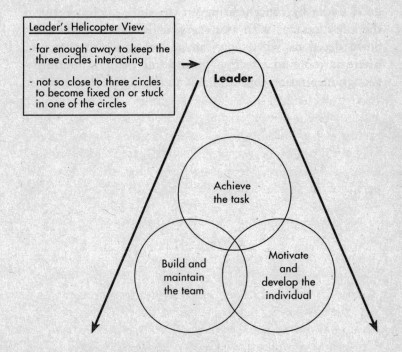

Figure 9.4 The Leadership Heliview

maintain an oversight of all three areas – TASK, TEAM and INDIVIDUAL – and how they are interacting or working together.

CONCLUSION

Of course it's a big mistake to see leadership solely in terms of motivating others. Leadership is also about giving direction in times of change. It is about building teams. Nor is motivation equated with vision and inspiration, though both have a part to play. Strive to become a very good leader by concentrating on the three circles. Perform the key functions with awareness, understanding and skill. Share decisions when you can and as much as you can. There is more to effective motivation than inspiration – though inspiration consummates all that a good leader does.

10

INSPIRING OTHERS

In their book *The Leadership Challenge* (1987) the Americans James Kouzes and Barry Posner identify five characteristics of what they call exemplary leaders:

- Leaders challenge the process. Leaders search for opportunities. They experiment and take risks, constantly challenging other people to exceed their own limitations.
- Leaders inspire a shared vision. Leaders envision an enabling future and enlist people to join in that new direction.
- Leaders enable others to act. Leaders strengthen others and foster collaboration.
- Leaders model the way. Leaders set the example for people by their own leadership behaviour and they plan small wins to get the process moving.
- Leaders encourage the heart. Leaders regard and recognize individual contributions and they celebrate team successes.

You will notice how often that word *inspire* crops up in the discussion of management these days, not least in the context of necessary leadership. The word is easy to say, isn't it? But how do you do it? *Can* you in fact learn to inspire others? Or is it one of those gifts of a natural or born leader? Certainly the ability to inspire others is the Mount Everest of motivation. Can you climb that mountain?

I cannot answer these questions for you. But in order to help you to think about them, this next chapter briefly outlines what is meant by inspiration. If nothing else it may serve to prevent the word *inspiration* joining all those other used, worn and discarded phrases on the rubbish dumps of management thought.

As the Italian proverb says, 'If you want clear water go back to the fountain-head.' The origin of our word *inspiration* is worth some reflection. It means literally to breathe into, from the Latin *spiritus* – breath, breathing, air. The old or primitive idea is that breath is life. Hence respiration. You see it in this literal sense in the Genesis story when: 'God formed man of dust from the ground, and breathed into his nostrils the breath of life; and man became a living being.'

In the Hebrew language the word for God's animating power or spirit was *ruach*, the same word used to describe the desert wind. The idea here is that God's spirit or breath could be breathed into people, such as the leaders and prophets of Israel. The Christian hymn 'Breathe on me breath of God, fill me with life anew' turns that metaphor into a prayer.

You will notice that in this scheme of things men and women are thought to have *spirits*, not unlike receiving sets. In other words, humans – some more than others – are capable of being infused or inspired by the divine spirit. But our spirits are not merely balloons or empty weather-vanes. They have an active life of their own, for good or ill.

Nowadays we are used to a division of the human being

into body and mind, with the latter held to be entirely a function or expression of the physical brain. In popular language, as a cultural legacy, we still distribute some of the brain's activities around the body. The heart, for example, is the seat of emotions (in ancient Israel they resided in the guts or stomach). Likewise a manager may refer to having a 'gut feeling' about a situation. We also continue to use the concept of *spirit* about individuals, teams and organizations. It suggests:

- the active or essential power operating in persons.
- a particular character, disposition or temper which exists in or pervades or animates a person or a group of persons.
- the disposition, feeling or frame of mind with which something is considered, viewed or done.
- a person, group or organization considered in relation to its character or disposition.
- the essential nature or qualities of someone or some group, which constitutes its pervading or tempering principles.

We can now begin to see why, as Lord Slim stated, leadership is concerned with the spiritual dimension. Although much of our motivation stems directly or indirectly from our bodies and their needs, a great deal more arises in our spirits.

THE EFFECTS OF INSPIRATION

Inspiration is not tangible but nonetheless it does exist and it does happen. Like electricity, which is also both real and invisible, inspiration can be seen by its effects. What are they?

In the Bible spirit seems originally to have been the idea of power supernatural or demonic, rather than strictly divine. Its operation was seen in all phenomena *in which people or creatures seemed to exceed their natural powers*, whether for good or evil. Spirit or *ruach* is responsible for the heroic feats of Samson, the wisdom of Joseph and the inspired utterances and deeds of the prophets.

Spirit, then, is active power or energy which invades people. It is superhuman, mysterious and elusive, like the wind of the desert that arises from nowhere and blows through the tents of the bedouin. Under its supernatural influence people go beyond the apparently set limits of human knowledge, physical powers or endurance, like rivers exceeding their banks. A cluster of words indicate this visible transcending or climbing across limits or barriers into a new country:

- EXCEED implies going beyond a limit set by *authority* or by *custom* or by *prior achievement*.
- SURPASS suggests superiority in quality, merit or skill.
- TRANSCEND implies a rising or extending notably above or beyond ordinary limits.
- EXCEL implies preeminence in achievement or quality and may suggest superiority to all others.

Notice that the concept of excellence, so central to business performance, comes from *excel* as defined above.

It looks as if people can be impelled or driven to ordinary levels of performance by natural motives, backed by fear or incentives. But to rise above or transcend accepted limits something more is needed – inspiration.

THE NELSON TOUCH

One important laboratory for studying inspiration is the battlefield. What can it tell us about this mysterious factor? The battlefield is both interesting and relevant in this respect because large numbers of men over many centuries have found themselves in more or less the same situation. They have always brought to it some natural fighting spirit. Those high spirits are often rapidly lowered by fear, anxiety, uncertainty and chaos. Yet sometimes soldiers transcend the expected limits. They perform extraordinary feats. Small numbers, like the 300 Spartans who held the pass at Thermopolae against a vast Persian host, can withstand much greater numbers – and sometimes overcome them. What is the secret?

Good leadership is one of them. As the Greek playwright Euripides wrote in the fourth century, 'Ten soldiers wisely led, will beat a hundred without a head.' But how does it work?

We must go back a step to the concept of spirit. It may be that spirit is the least individualistic or particular of all our attributes. It may be in us, so to speak, but it is not of us. We do not own it. Consequently we may be much more susceptible to influence at this level. We are also capable of exerting influences or sending 'radio waves', which other spirits or the common pool of spirit will feel.

If that is the case you can see that a 'master spirit' living and working among people could have an influence out of all proportion to what might be expected. This effect will be greatly heightened if there are unique conditions – such as the fear and uncertainty of war – that make spirits especially sensitive to influence.

'I never saw a man in our profession . . . who possessed the magic art of infusing the same spirit into others which inspired their own actions . . . all agree there is but one Nelson.'

Admiral Lord St Vincent, writing to Nelson

Hope is the oxygen of the human spirit. By building up the self-confidence and pride of others on the one hand and by inspiring confidence in you as a leader, manager or professional – especially in the plan you propose – you have infused or breathed some hope into a situation where before there may have been only depression, despondency, growing apathy and even despair, the black hole from which no hope ever escapes. Can you do more?

HOW TO INSPIRE OTHERS

Yes. After informing and convincing people about what needs to be done and persuading them that none of it is impossible, you may then be able sometimes to renew their vision. Why are we going through this struggle together? Why is it worthwhile? Remember, as Martin Luther once said, 'Everything that is done in this world is by hope.'

These questions or issues are especially acute for soldiers, among others, for they may be called upon to surrender their lives. In exchange for what? What is the great hope that animates the human spirit. Victory? Yes, but victory to what end? As a leader you have to be able to communicate in clear, simple and vivid language your answer to that fundamental question – what is it all for?

Dimly, as through a frosted glass, we can see that in order to inspire us a vision must be more than demanding or challenging. It must give us the seeds of hope that in some way or other by our efforts – however modest – we are creating a better world for our families and for humanity.

THE ENEMY WITHIN

By far the most dangerous foe we have to fight is *apathy* – indifference from whatever cause; not from lack of knowledge, but from carelessness, from absorption in other pursuits, from a contempt bred of self-satisfaction.

Sir William Osler

Not all so-called visions, then, are capable of inspiring people. To be inspiring a vision has to appeal to the inherent nobility within us. It has to be capable of exalting the mind and animating the spirit. 'There is no money in poetry,' once mused Robert Frost, but, he added, 'neither is there any poetry in money.'

CONCLUSION

There is no inspiration in the ideals of plenty or stability. No one will ever be inspired by the aim of making you and your fellow shareholder even richer. Go back to your common task and dig deeper until you find the clear water at the bottom of the well. It is that water which refreshes the human spirit.

11

THE FIFTY-FIFTY PRINCIPLE

As a leader, both individually and as a member of the leadership team of the organization for which you work, you should be willing to accept the full responsibility for motivation. In your relations with your partners – all those who work in that organization – the Golden Rule of 'doing unto others as you would have them do to you' is a good guide – as long as you remember that the *initiative* lies with you.

BUILDING THE HIGH-PERFORMANCE TEAM

In other words, you are accountable for the motivation and morale of your team. Every member should, like you, have a *sense of responsibility* for the three circles, and for transforming the team into a high-performance one. Such a team will be, by definition, well motivated. It should have the following hallmarks:

- Sets clear realistic objectives
- Shares a sense of purpose
- Uses resources well

- Maintains atmosphere of openness
- Reviews own progress
- Builds on experience
- Rides out storms
-
-

That list isn't exhaustive, and I have left two spaces blank for you to add to the characteristics from your own experience.

It's important for you to be clear about this list. For you will be judged ultimately as a business leader not by your personal qualities however attractive, not by your professional or technical knowledge, not by whether or not you have read every book on management under the sun, but *by your fruits*.

THE REAL TEST

'You will know them by their fruits. Are grapes gathered from thorns, or figs from thistles? So, every sound tree bears good fruit, but the bad tree bears evil fruit. A sound tree cannot bear evil fruit, nor can a bad tree bear good fruit. Every tree that does not bear good fruit is cut down and thrown into the fire. Thus you will know them by their fruits.'

Matthew Chapter 7.

And the chief fruit or by-product of your leadership is the calibre or quality of the team you create. By their fruits – the teams they create – you will know if you have leaders working for you.

It all starts here — with your vision of what a high-performance team should look like.

By *shared sense of purpose* I don't mean that everyone should be able to recite together the organizational mission Statement. I mean ENERGY. All that the team does is done with purpose. The energies of each individual have become the team's synergy — the corporate energy or *esprit de corps* which is more than the sum of its parts.

WHERE THE FAULT LIES

Have you noticed the human tendency among managers to keep the credit for themselves and pass the blame down the line?

It's all too easy to blame *others* for poor results, indifferent performance and total lack of interest.

'You should see the people who work for me,' Henry Goldberg told me, 'and then you would understand what I am up against. They are lazy, idle and just don't seem to care. They do just enough work to avoid getting dismissed. They need a bomb under them to wake them up. I have criticized them individually in their appraisal interviews, reprimanded them, punished them, offered them incentives — nothing works. It's just my bad luck, I suppose, to get landed with such a bunch of useless people. Last week they even threatened to strike because I keep losing my temper and swearing at them. They even had the nerve to suggest that I don't set a good example. What should I do?'

The Fifty-Fifty Principle, as I shall call it, suggests an antidote to this frustration. It invites you (and Henry

Goldberg) to look in the mirror first at yourself and your own leadership – or lack of it – before criticizing the motivation of others.

> Fifty per cent of motivation comes from within a person and fifty per cent from his or her environment, especially from the leadership encountered there.

Motivation, we can confidently conclude from Part One, largely comes from within a person in response to his or her inner and unfolding programme of needs, desires, ambitions and values. But the various stimuli that come from outside the person in the ever-changing social environment, particularly from the leadership within it, are vitally important.

A child, for example, might have a potential interest in science and be generally ambitious to do well at school and go to university. But the Fifty-Fifty Principle comes into play. Fifty per cent of the child's progress will depend upon the academic quality of the school and in particular upon the personality and ability of the science teacher. A great schoolteacher has been defined as 'one whose actual lessons may be forgotten, but whose living enthusiasm is a quickening, animating and inspiring power'.

The Fifty-Fifty Principle does have the benefit of reminding leaders that they have a key part to play – for good or ill – in the motivation of people at work. Fortunately (or unfortunately) not all the cards are in their hands, for they are dealing with people who are self-motivating in various degrees. The art of leadership is to work with the natural grain of the particular wood of humanity which comes to hand.

There is also a valuable teaching element in the Fifty-

Fifty Principle. You may recall the old proverb, 'There are no bad soldiers, only bad officers.' Now as a statement this is not really true. There *are* bad soldiers. But it's a very good maxim to teach young officers, for it puts them on their mettle. It invites them to examine themselves and their own leadership before blaming the troops. Thus it inoculates them against one form of rationalization.

NO BAD STUDENTS ...

Two boys who appeared with Katharine Hepburn in the film *Olly Olly Oxen Free* were initially awed by her, but she instinctively put them at ease. On the third day of production, one of the boys forgot his lines and Hepburn said, 'My fault, my fault.' The boy asked, 'How could it be your fault? I forgot the line.' She replied, 'Because I delivered *my* line too fast. That made you forget.'

Ellen Peck and Dr William Ganzig in *The Parent Test*

LOOK HOMEWARDS FIRST

The Fifty-Fifty Principle does not claim to identify the different proportions in the equation exactly. It is more like a rough-and-ready rule of thumb. In effect it says no more than that a substantial part of motivation lies within us while a substantial part lies, so to speak, outside and beyond our control. Above all, it will act as a spur to you (if you need any more goading in this direction!) to get your 50 per cent right as a leader and manager before you start complaining about the poor motivation or low morale of others.

> One day when the fleet was at sea the officer on watch reported to Admiral Collingwood, Nelson's great friend, that a meeting was about to break out among the 800 sailors on the ship. 'A meeting on my ships!' exclaimed Collingwood. 'If that is the case then it's the fault of myself and every one of my officers.'

Such stories invite us to look within – at the state of our own inner leadership – before we storm onto the deck and blame the crew. Only when you have taken the beam out of your own eye will you be able to see in order to remove the speck from your neighbour's eye.

If there is an industrial strike how many chief executives and managers would begin like Collingwood by blaming themselves and questioning their collective leadership? 'If you are not part of the solution you are part of the problem.' The Fifty-Fifty Principle is an invitation to get your part in the motivational relationship right.

Doubtless other applications of the Fifty-Fifty Principle will soon be discovered. As I have already mentioned in *Effective Teambuilding* (1986), it applies to the relative values of leadership and teamwork: fifty per cent of success depends on the team and fifty per cent on the leader. Again these are not scientific proportions. But they do indicate just how substantial is each contribution, regardless of that made by the other party. Here the Fifty-Fifty Principle challenges the leader (or team or individual team member) to get his or her part right first before criticizing the quality or contribution of the other party. It is the ultimate cure to the 'Us and Them' disease of organizations.

We could apply the same principle to the Nature versus Nurture debate. About half our destiny depends upon inherited characteristics or tendencies; the other half depends upon what we (or others) make of them. In the second part of that proposition lies the real challenge to parents and teachers. Certainly that applies in the leadership field. The idea that leaders are born and not made is a half-truth. The full truth is that they are (about) half born and (more-or-less) half made – by experience and thought, by training and practice. This mixture of self-teaching and teaching by others of course takes a lifetime. For paradoxically it takes a long time to become a natural leader.

What moves us to action may come from within or from without, or – more commonly – from some combination of inner impulse or proclivity on the one hand and outer situations or stimuli on the other. The merit of *motivation* as a word is that it fits perfectly the Fifty-Fifty Principle. For it covers both what happens inside an individual in terms of wanting to do something and also what happens outside them as they are influenced by others or by circumstances. When someone is motivating you, he or she is consciously or unconsciously seeking to change the strength and/or direction of your motive energy.

ROGER PENSKE –
AMERICAN MOTOR RACING TEAM BOSS

On 16 April 1994 Al Unser Junior, driving for Marlboro Team Penske, won the third race of the US Indy Car Series at Long Beach, California. The American TV commentator had this to say about team boss, Roger Penske, during Unser's final lap:

'Roger fuels himself on winning. If he wins he becomes

obsessed with winning more. There's nobody like Roger Penske in the racing world, and history will always show that he's an individual who nobody else has ever come close to.

'Without Roger's motivation, without his drive, without his strong desire, everybody in the team would probably be only 50% of what they are.'

This reminds me of 50–50 motivation!

This second aspect of motivation, incidentally, does raise again the ethical issue. As I have suggested above, we are actually dependent in varying degrees upon outside stimulation of various kinds in all aspects of our mental life, not least our motivation. But this human dependency on others can be used for our own ends. How does the legitimate and proper motivation of others differ from manipulation?

To manipulate someone means to control or play upon them by artful, unfair or insidious means, especially to one's own advantage. Therefore there are two aspects of manipulation: the means and the ends. If it is *your* purpose and not a *common* purpose that is being served, you are running into the danger of manipulation. If the means you employ to motivate others are hidden from them or seek to bypass their conscious minds, then you are becoming a manipulator rather than a motivator.

Motivating others, therefore, should not be confused with manipulatory practices used by strong personalities to dominate weaker ones. Leadership exists in its most natural form among equals. It is not the same as domination or the exercise of power. True leaders respect the integrity of others. Bosses demand respect; leaders give respect. Granted such a relationship, based upon mutual trust and supported by a common sense of justice or fairness, then it is part of the responsibility of leaders to stir up enthusiasm for the common task.

CONCLUSION

A key indicator of your success as a leader is your ability to create and maintain a high-performance team. That team will have certain characteristics or hallmarks, among them a shared sense of purpose. By definition, then, it's highly motivated. New members are soon infected by its common spirit or *esprit de corps*, just as a green stick in a bundle of dry wood will soon burn merrily on the fire.

It is easy to blame others or circumstances or bad luck if you fail to create such a team or organization. But remember the Fifty-Fifty Principle! Make doubly sure that you have got right your 50 per cent of the equation first before you start castigating others. So often relations between managers and their subordinates can resemble those between Adam and Eve after their expulsion from Eden as captured in the eye of John Milton:

'Thus they in mutual accusation spent the fruitless hours, neither self-condemning.' Break out of that vicious circle of recrimination by boldly and publicly shouldering your responsibility for the present state of affairs – and then asking the others to help you to restore harmony and create greatness. You will not be disappointed.

But *how* do you fulfil your 50 per cent of the new psychological contract so that it overflows? The seven strategies in Part Three may serve as your vectors, or compass bearings.

THE SERVANT LEADER

A leader is best
when people barely know that he exists,
not so good when people obey and proclaim him,
worst when they despise him.
Fail to honour people,
they fail to honour you.
But of a leader who talks little,
when his work is done, his aim fulfilled,
they will say, 'we did this ourselves.'

And perhaps one day they will add – 'But you as our leader made the vital difference.'

HOW TO DRAW OUT THE BEST FROM PEOPLE

The next seven chapters focus on the main strategies that you should adopt if you wish to draw out the best from everyone at work – including yourself. I have called them STRATEGIES because they are the really IMPORTANT things you have to do. Also because most of them will involve your ORGANIZATION as well as yourself.

These key STRATEGIES are:

- be motivated yourself
- select people who are already motivated
- set challenging but realistic targets
- remember that progress motivates
- treat each person as an individual
- provide fair rewards
- give recognition

Part Three is essentially concerned with what works in practice. Therefore I have married the much wider tradition of human experience across the centuries to the insights and summaries of common sense that have emerged from theory or research.

By the time you have finished reading and working on Part Three you should:

1. be able to identify the seven main STRATEGIES that together give you and your organization a clear sense of direction towards creating high-performance teamwork.

2. know what SKILLS you can develop in each of these seven strategic areas of importance.

3. as far as your ORGANIZATION is concerned, be better equipped to act as a change-agent, as it seeks to transform itself into a more stimulating and motivating environment.

12

BE MOTIVATED YOURSELF

One of the world's first philosopher consultants, Confucius, was once called in by a Chinese feudal king to check the corruption and theft which was rife in his domain. The fact that both the king and his court indulged in these practices, and that others were taking their cue from them, soon became apparent to Confucius, and he simply pointed out to his client the motivating influence – for good or ill – of example. 'If you did not steal yourself,' he said, 'even if you rewarded men with gold to steal they would not do it.'

The first and golden rule of motivation is that you will never inspire others unless you are inspired yourself. Only a motivated leader motivates others. Example is the great seducer.

It is so simple and so obvious, isn't it? But why is it so neglected in management today?

Enthusiasm inspires, especially when combined with trust. Its key importance can perhaps best be seen by considering its opposites. What impression would we make as leaders if we were apathetic, stolid, half-hearted, indifferent and uninterested? Enthusiasm is infectious; and enthusiasts are usually competent too, since they believe in and like what they are doing.

Before you criticize others for lack of motivation ask yourself if your own enthusiasm for and commitment to the task in hand is sincere, visible and tangible. Have you expressed it in deeds as well as words? Are you setting a good example? For motivation is a virus: it is caught, not taught.

PROVIDE A GOOD EXAMPLE

We all know from experience the power of the example of others on our own motivation. If a leader is enthusiastic and motivated it is contagious.

EXERCISE

Can you identify any leader who has inspired or motivated you?
What characteristics did they have?
Conversely, can you think of an incident where bad example set by a manager reduced the energy and motivation of the group?

Many managers, if they were honest, would have to admit they are like the character in Shakespeare's *Merchant of Venice* who declared: 'I can easier teach twenty what were good to be done, than be one of the twenty to follow my own teaching.'

It is best to think of example as something you provide rather than set. Setting an example suggests a conscious intention to do something for effect. Shouldn't example spring out of what you are and what you believe, regardless of effect?

Public	Don't hide your light. Act in the open.
Spontaneous	Example is best when it is perceived as spontaneous, not calculated. Let it happen naturally.
Expressive	Leadership should be YOU. Don't do things for effect – do them because it's natural for you. Why does the bird sing?
Self-Effacing	Good example shouldn't draw attention to itself. It is not self-seeking. No trumpets!

Figure 12.1   Hallmarks of Good Example

You may disagree with me that good example shouldn't be consciously calculated. But in my experience doing things for effect can be counter-productive. In this context it's a fairly academic point, because you can't *simulate* energetic purposefulness, enthusiasm or drive. If those around you are to see and feel it in you then it has to be really there.

As an example of this unselfconscious example let me quote the impression that General Wavell made on his officers at the time when his whole command in the Far East was disintegrating early in 1942. 'We had all seen him breasting adversity,' his senior staff officer has written, 'but none of us had seen him downcast, or heard him repine. He never kept up a front in our presence; what we saw of him was the full, the genuine character; and the more we saw of it, the more aware we became of its flawlessness.'

By providing example here you fulfil your side of a bargain. In Part One I introduced the idea that there is — or should be — an equivalence in our relations with each other. If you do this for me then I will do that for you. This equivalence may often need to be written down in contracts, but often much is left implicit. If both parties understand and consent to these implicit exchanges, shadowed by expectations, then their relation will serve well its end. For example, I once heard a woman say 'if you treat me as a woman I will treat you as a man.' That may sound very basic common sense.

In the relation of leader and colleagues there is a similar equivalence at work. While I was serving as the adjutant of a Bedouin regiment in the Arab Legion I stayed in a Bedouin black tent far out in the desert. Around the fire that night, as the brass coffee pot sizzled on the embers, the sheikh of that tribe quoted an Arab proverb that has lived in my mind:

GIVE ME A FIRE AND I WILL GIVE YOU LIGHT

It sums up for me that one element in an almost spiritual contract. It exists between leaders and their partners, who know their need for each other. Incidentally, I have put the proverb in capitals because it is worth carving it over your mantelpiece, if not on your heart.

As a leader you mustn't expect your team and individuals to produce LIGHT unless you contribute FIRE. You cannot motivate anyone unless you are motivated yourself. In this respect, wear your heart on your sleeve so that all can see who you are, where you are coming from and where you are going.

HOW NOT TO DO IT

Once I spoke at a conference in Singapore for a hundred senior managers of a major international pharmaceutical company. It was their second attempt at launching a new 'total quality' and 'empowerment' programme, together with some 'business process reengineering'. Not only was the new approach not fully understood, but it had yet to be enthusiastically led by the senior executives. It soon became clear that one of the prime causes for the lack of motivation could be traced back to one person. The key executive vice-president responsible for the innovation had been made redundant shortly after the first conference. He was then asked back on a three-month contract just to initiate the new strategy. He was not exactly motivated himself.

Commitment is strong motivation that has passed through the junctions of your conscious mind and the signal box of your will; it moves through firm decision and into action. Such a commitment releases new energies. It's as if the forces of your personality align themselves into a new magnetic field. The very act of choosing throws a new element into the picture, like a stone thrown into a pond. The configuration is changed, if ever so slightly. You have thrown your weight on one side or other. The balance tilts. This is the creative and the dynamic element in decision.

BEGIN IT NOW

Until one is committed
there is hesitancy, the chance to draw back,
always ineffectiveness.
Concerning all acts of initiative (and creation)
there is one elementary truth
the ignorance of which kills countless ideas
and splendid plans.
That the moment one definitely commits
oneself
then Providence moves too
All sorts of things occur to help one
that would never otherwise have occurred
A whole stream of events issues from the
decision
raising in one's favour all manner
of unforeseen incidents and meetings
and material assistance
Which no man could have dreamt
would have come his way.
Whatever you can do or dream you can
begin it
Boldness has genius, power and magic in it
Begin it now.

                                        Goethe

BE COMMITTED – AND SHOW IT

Commitment suggests a decision from which there is no turning back or possibility of repeat.

> In 1066 Duke William of Normandy landed on the southern shores of England as an invader. He knew that shortly the whole military force of the Anglo-Saxons would concentrate to crush his small army of Normans. William ordered all the ships that had transported his soldiers across the Channel to be burnt. He wanted a committed army, highly motivated to win when the only alternative was death in battle or to be driven back into the sea. The Normans won.

Notice that in this story Duke William now shared the same danger as his men – the hallmark of leadership.

Committed leaders begin to show those qualities most associated with motivation. In adversity they show tenacity and resolve. They are single-minded. You will not find it easy to deflect them from their purpose. 'I am not made to despair – what men can do shall be done,' wrote Nelson to Lord Melville during the long pursuit of the French Toulon fleet in 1805. Before Badajoz four years later Wellington wrote to one of his officers, 'As it is, however, I do not despair. I have in hand a most difficult task from which I may not extricate myself; but I must not shrink from it.'

Of course such perseverance has to be balanced with flexibility. Whether to persist with a course of action that isn't working too well or to switch to an alternative may require considerable judgement on your part as a leader. 'A foolish consistency', wrote Emerson, 'is the hobgoblin of little minds.'

Putting it another way, real commitment begins to transform you. You cannot go back and jump the other way. It's too late. You will be a different person. If you wish to be a transformational leader rather than a transactional manager, it starts here with your willingness to change yourself through a greater commitment. As Gandhi once said, 'We must be the change we wish to see in the world.'

In terms of motivating others your own commitment is vital. For it is the key that opens the prison door of self. You begin to give yourself – to the common task, to the team, and to the individual who needs your help or guidance. As says the French proverb, 'He gives nothing who does not give himself.'

ARE YOU IN THE RIGHT JOB?

Remember that you'll have extreme difficulty in carrying out these principles if you aren't in the right job. You have found your vocation if your natural energies flow easily into your work. If you aren't very motivated it may mean that you are not yet in the right field of work. If this proves to be the case you will not be able to motivate others. You are like a racehorse falling at the first fence. Check yourself immediately against the following symptoms of being in the wrong job:

- You have little or no interest in the work itself.
- You have a sense of being 'a square peg in a round hole'.
- You avoid talking about work.
- You actively dislike a significant part of the job.
- You arrive late and leave early.
- You constantly look forward to being able to leave.

In contrast to this dismal picture you should feel that you have found your vocation. By that I don't mean that the heavens opened and a voice said 'Become a manager!' or 'Become a laywer!'. Rather, by self-knowledge, judgement, trial-and-error and perhaps a lot of luck, you have found the best way you can of using your particular talents, interests and personality. Your work will use all the colours on your palette. It will still feel like work, but it won't be toil or drudgery. It should be fun. For you will enjoy it as much, if not more, than anything else you do. If you have such a sense of a vocation you may have many problems, but surely motivation will not be one of them.

Well, perhaps that isn't quite true. Perhaps there is an element of toil or hard labour in every job. 'It is not a paradox to assert that man often dislikes the work which he likes,' Arnold Bennett once said in a conversation with a fellow writer. 'For myself, every day anew, I hate to start work.'

Long after the ape and tiger in our human nature have faded back into jungle, there will remain the donkey. That most intractable and enduring animal will always, for example, do the minimum if left to its own discretion. It is naturally lazy. Sometimes we have to persuade that beloved but idle donkey within us to move forwards. Promises of carrots or little prods with a stick usually work.

A PERSONAL IMPERATIVE

Do what you, and no one else, feel that you were meant to do, what to you is a sufficient reward for the labour and sweat because it occupies your interest and intrigues your imagination. If you want to paint pictures . . . if you don't you won't be a whole man.

Lyndall Urwick

CHECKLIST: ARE YOU IN THE RIGHT WORK?

Whether you have five, two or one talents you should know
what they are. Then you can choose work which uses and
develops your natural abilities.

	Yes	No
Do you really enjoy your work at present, taking it as a whole?	❑	❑
Would you say that you had one outstanding talent which you could name instantly?	❑	❑
Have others recognized that talent by such means as commendation, reward or promotion?	❑	❑
Did you discover it before you were 25 years old? (Specific talents usually make an early appearance)	❑	❑
Can you identify the key natural abilities of		
(a) your best friend	❑	❑
(b) your superior manager	❑	❑
(c) each of your team members	❑	❑
Does your present work both extend and develop your aptitudes?	❑	❑
Would you take a lower salary or fee if some work offered to you was specifically appropriate to your knowledge and skill?	❑	❑
Have you ever paid out of your own pocket to go on a course that would sharpen and develop your chief natural ability?	❑	❑

THE LEADER'S DEEPER RESOURCES

'Leaders have to motivate and inspire others, but where do leaders find their inspiration?' asked a senior manager at a conference on leadership recently. How would you have answered her question?

Flora Robson, a great British actress, once said: 'Only God can inspire.' Now it is true that many leaders are religious in the sense that they look to some power outside or beyond themselves. 'The greatest leaders have been sustained by a belief that they were in some way instruments of destiny,' wrote Ordway Tead in *The Art of Leadership* (1934), 'that they tapped hidden reserves of power, that they truly lived as they tried to live in harmony with some greater, more universal purpose or intention in the world.' Perhaps it is on the odd occasions when we see and hear leaders who are aligned with that universal purpose that we find them inspiring.

It seems necessary, in short, that as a leader you 'should believe in some meaning in human living, in some fruitful outcome of human effort, in some sense that humanity struggles not against but essentially in harmony with the animating power of the universe. The best leader,' Ordway Tead continues, 'has faith in the world as a place where there is a real better and worse, where these are ascertainable, and where effort towards the good can yield appreciable results. Only when a leader has such a faith does he or she possess the essence of the deepest inspiration which people crave from them.'

You cannot give unless you receive. What wells of inspiration have you identified in your life?

EXERCISE

Can you think of a person you have met in the last three months who has said something that you found inspiring?

Who do you think is the most inspiring person in the world today?

What books do you read that contain inspiration as well as information?

Have you read any story in the newspaper or seen any on television in the last week that uplifted your spirit?

Remember that you can always share or pass on such touches of the spirit as you have received. There's no copyright on the thoughts of God. They are the pollen you transmute into your own spoken words and actions. The prize is a great one: to be able to inspire others with the same spirit that inspires you. But, as the poet Robert Browning once said: 'It's no good trying to shine if you don't take time to fill your lamp.'

CHECKLIST: ARE YOU MOTIVATED YOURSELF?

	Yes	No
Do you feel enthusiastic and committed about the work you are doing?	☐	☐
Which of the following has used the words 'enthusiastic' or 'committed' about you in the last three months?		
a superior	☐	☐
a colleague	☐	☐
a team member	☐	☐

When things go wrong do you tend to take
responsibility yourself rather than blame others? ❏ ❏

Can you identify three ways in which you lead by
example? ❏ ❏

Do you act on the Fifty-Fifty Principle?
Always ❏   Sometimes ❏   Seldom ❏

Are you clear about the distinction between
motivating others by word and example, as
opposed to trying to manipulate them? ❏ ❏

Does the example you set spring from within you,
as opposed to being done for calculated effect? ❏ ❏

Do you give up easily? ❏ ❏

Are you sure that you are working in the right field
for your interests, abilities and temperament? ❏ ❏

Have you ever experienced an occasion when
something you said or did clearly had an
inspirational influence on another individual, a team
or an organization? ❏ ❏

KEY POINTS

- The cornerstone of motivating others is to *be motivated yourself*. For motivation is like a virus – it's contagious.

- Your enthusiasm, commitment and perseverance in the face of difficulty are three badges of leadership. The next time you look in a mirror, ask yourself if the face that you see expresses these qualities. Then add a smile. As the Chinese proverb says, 'If you cannot smile do not open your shop today.'

- 'There are no bad soldiers, only bad officers.' That's not strictly true. There *are* bad soldiers (students, staff, workers, etc.). But only about five in every hundred. The other 95 people in every hundred are on your side. It's *your* fault if they are not fully committed. At least that is what the Fifty-Fifty Principle teaches us.

- Never ask others to do what you are not willing to do yourself. Good example gives you the only real influence over others that you are likely to have. It also gives you the moral authority to ask for sacrifice.

- If you aren't strongly motivated yourself, don't despair. It may be a symptom that you are in the wrong line of work. If it's not too late, make a change. For your own energies need to flow freely in what you are doing.

- Inspiration depends on a number of factors – the chemistry of those involved, the nature of the task, and the situation. But, given the right circumstances, your words and example can put a torch to the dry wood. Be prepared to experience moments of inspiration – when you say or do just the right thing.

Nothing great was ever achieved without enthusiasm.

Emerson

13

SELECT PEOPLE WHO ARE ALREADY MOTIVATED

'You have founded a most successful business. Everyone I have met this morning seems highly motivated. What is your secret?' This is the question I put to Dmitro Comino, the entrepreneur and manager who created a company called Dexion. I had spent that morning seeing just how good Dexion – makers of high-quality shelving – was as a team. It was most impressive.

'Secret?' replied Comino. 'What do you mean?'

'How do you motivate those who aren't especially keen? Most managers find that very hard to do.'

Comino was a natural thinker about management, some-one who thought for himself from first principles – not out of textbooks. He paused to reflect.

'Yes, it's very difficult,' he finally agreed. 'That is why I suggest that they avoid the problem. *Select people who are already motivated.*'

You may call that a mere flash of common sense, but it illuminated the whole subject of motivation for me. Of course!

From the Fifty-Fifty Principle it follows that the extent to which you can motivate anyone else is limited. For 50 per cent of the cards are, so to speak, in their hands. You can provide motives or incentives in one way or another; you can offer rewards or issue threats; you can attempt to persuade. All these actual or potential influences may have an effect, for remember that 50 per cent of a person's motivation stems from the environment. If you are a manager-leader, then you are a key factor in the environment of those that work for you. But your power is limited. As the proverb says, 'You can take a horse to water, but you cannot make him drink.'

Since it is so hard to motivate people who are not already motivated it makes sense to select those who already are. It is true that in the coldest flint there is hot fire, but you may lack the personality or skill to release such hidden sparks. Perhaps if they had worked on Nelson's ship they would become infused by his spirit. But you don't happen to be Nelson. Like all of us you have to row with the oars you have received. A proper sense of your own limitations, not a false modesty, should lead you to avoid attempting to climb that Everest of inspiring those whom no one else can inspire — at least until you have worn in your climbing boots on lesser mountains.

EACH TEAM MEMBER MATTERS

'What do you do about selecting motivated people?' I asked the Director of Human Resources of a major international company. His eyes lit up.

'We take immense pains, John, to get the right people.' He checked some figures on his desk computer screen. 'Last year we spent just over a million dollars on head-hunters. We also have five managers at Group Head Office here who specialize in management recruitment. Would you like to see how we select our graduate entry?'

'You have perhaps misunderstood me,' I replied, 'doubtless because I haven't made myself clear. I am really interested in how you select people for the *whole* organization – all the 4000 people who work here – not just the top two hundred business executives.'

The light faded in his eyes.

'I am not too sure about that now. Anyway it's all done at local level. In the division in which I worked as a personnel director four or five years ago we used to advertise and hire those who had the right technical skills. We did have quite a big labour turnover problem, but so did every other company in that part of the world. Mercifully the recession has cured that problem for us.'

Organizations like this one still think in hierarchical ways. All the money available for selecting and training goes to the apex of the hierarchy. We need to reverse the pyramid. Much of the same care that goes into selecting the managers should be invested in choosing every member of the team.

Rolleron Ltd is a small company employing 80 people making diary and commercial gift products. It had a vacancy in a new product team for a specialist in direct mail. Apart from a marketing background and computer skills, the product manager was looking for someone who could work well in the team and be flexible about their contribution as the work expanded.

The three short-listed candidates were all interviewed by the team leader and his sales and marketing director. Each of the three were then invited to give a presentation to these two, now joined by the managing director, on how they would develop the customer data base and use it in a new marketing strategy. Especial attention was payed to their motivation and willingness to commit themselves to Rolleron's vision for the exciting new product.

In the old days the motivation of the work force, as it was called, didn't much matter. Subordinates did what the boss told them to do – or not to do. Thinking was not a required skill. Training consisted of inculcating drills and work habits. This approval reached its climax in the armies of the world, the very models for large industrial and commercial organizations as they came into being during the last century.

THE PRUSSIAN SOLDIER

'As to the common men, the leading idea of the Prussian discipline is to reduce them, in many respects, to the nature of machines; that they may have no volition of their own, but be actuated solely by that of their officers; that they may have such a superlative dread of those officers as annihilates all fear of the enemy; and that they may move forwards when ordered, without deeper reasoning or more concern than the muskets they carry along with them.'

John Moore, *A View of Society and Manners in France, Switzerland and Germany* (1793)

Even in the military field, however, the best minds from time immemorial have known that quality matters, not quantity. Quality of leadership and quality of soldiers too – especially the presence of intelligence and inner motivation.

You may remember the story in the Bible when God tells Gideon that 'The people with you are too many for me to give the Midianites into their hand . . . Now, therefore, proclaim in the ears of the people, saying, "whoever is fearful and trembling, let him return home."' After Gideon had put that test only 10,000 out of 32,000 stayed with him. But they were still too many for God's liking. Gideon was now commanded to take them down to the water; he was told to send back to their tents those who lay prostrated in order to drink. He was directed, by contrast, to keep with him those who lapped the water with their tongues like dogs. For, we may surmise, they maintained a soldier-like vigilance: they put the task before their individual needs. After that final selection test Gideon was left with only 300 men – fully motivated and natural soldiers. With them he defeated the host of Midianites.

You need people working for you who, like John Bunyan, 'could not be content, unless I was found in the exercise of my gift, unto which also I was greatly animated.' Bunyan added that 'great grace and small gifts are better than great gifts and no grace', which can be translated here to mean that when you select someone for a job a high motivation and modest talent is to be preferred to considerable talent but little or no evidence of motivation.

When John Bunyan was a pikeman in the army of Parliament during the English Civil War its greatest military leader was Oliver Cromwell. Like many others of his generation, caught up in that bitter civil war, he had to teach himself cavalry tactics after he was more than forty years old. He found within himself the gift of leadership; the seeds of his success as a leader lay in his acute observation of human nature. He watched how the spirited Cavaliers, inspired by honour and loyalty, easily crushed in battle the 'decayed servingmen and tapsters' who peopled the Parliamentarian cavalry – men who often served only for wages. They could never equal Cavaliers. Cromwell determined to select only those who were motivated by the cause:

> 'Give me the red-coated captain,' Cromwell said, 'who knows what he is fighting for and loves what he knows.'

Cromwell applied the same principle to all ranks. His famous regiment soon acquired a reputation for being invincible – the Ironsides, as their Cavalier opponents called them.

HOW TO IDENTIFY MOTIVATION IN OTHERS

In the above example religious zeal played a large part. But there are other kinds of zeal or enthusiasm. In today's world you should indeed look for those who love what they are doing – or have the capacity to fall in love with it. There are usually some clear indicators if you have eyes to see them.

ATTRIBUTE	SYMPTOMS
Energy	Does this person convey a sense of energy? It may not be displayed in an extrovert way. More a certain alertness and quiet resolve.

Commitment	Is this person still wavering? Is he or she already committed – or willing to commit – to the common purpose?
Staying Power	Starting journeys together is easy. But what happens when we face the first problems, obstacles, difficulties? Who will turn back or give up too easily?
Skill	The skills that people have acquired are usually good signposts to the direction in which they want to travel.
Single-Mindedness	'Those who attain any excellence,' wrote Dr Samuel Johnson, 'commonly spend life in one pursuit; for excellence is not often granted upon easier terms.' Don't choose a dilettante or a butterfly. Power comes from energy applied in a single direction.
Enjoyment	People who don't enjoy their work – or find moments of joy in it – are unlikely to be highly motivated.
Responsibility	A willingness to accept and seek responsibility is a sure symptom of a well-motivated person.

Figure 13.1.   Indicators of High Motivation

Keep that Fifty-Fifty Principle always in mind. If someone you recruit is a poor performer or leaves you without adequate reason *it's your fault*. You made an error of judgement. Perhaps you put someone into a position too challenging for them. Or you misread his or her natural talents or abilities. Hope has its victories, but don't let it triumph too often over common sense or experience.

By ENJOYMENT in the table above I don't mean hilarity or a 'laugh a minute'. Some work offers only tears, not laughter. Seeds of enjoyment can lie in the rocks themselves or even under ice. 'When men and women are rightly occupied,' wrote John Ruskin, 'their amusement grows out of their work, like petals out of a fruitful flower.' If someone you have appointed does not find the work interesting, enjoyable, entertaining, amusing or fun – and you don't hear mention of these words when that person talks to others about the job – I am afraid you have chosen the wrong person. I needn't tell you now who to blame.

EXERCISE

You are the leader of a university expedition setting out to explore a remote plateau in the Venezuelan rain forest. You have one place left in your team and three people have expressed interest. You need a botanist.

MIKE is an older postgraduate botanist, very well qualified. He wants to buy a house, as he is recently engaged to be married. He has been on three expeditions before, but now thinks he ought to settle down. Yet he is tempted by this particular plateau . . .

SALLY wants to specialize in tropical medicine and in particular obtaining new drugs from rare plants. She is still a medical student but is willing to sell her car in order to come.

JANE has already helped with fund-raising. She is willing to work as a waitress to raise her own contribution, and will do literally anything to come including attending a course at the Institute of Tropical Botany.

Who do you think you will select? What three questions would you ask each of the three?

Selecting the right people is largely a matter of judgement, spiced with intuition. The following model is a reminder of the essentials you are having to consider and weigh in the balances of your judgement. Remember the old saying in the antique trade that you make your profit or loss when you buy the goods. So look carefully at:

Figure 13.2   The Motivation Triangle.

Motivation	Those aspects of life and work that bring a sense of enjoyment, satisfaction, fulfilment
Ability	Experience, skills, knowledge
Personality	How we fit in with people and situations

You will never get it right every time. But always learn the lessons from your errors or mistakes. A fool is someone who goes on making the same mistakes. You can usually diagnose your shortcomings as a judge under one or other of those headings: MOTIVATION, ABILITY, PERSONALITY.

Here are some useful tips:

- Remember that someone at an interview is trying to influence or motivate you to give them the job. Some people find it easy to *act* as if they are highly motivated or enthusiastic for an hour during an interview. Others, who may be very motivated, may come across as 'laid back'.

- By their fruits you shall know them. Look for evidence in what they have done. What someone wishes to do he or she will find a way of doing. Have persistence and perseverance – evidences of high motivation – ever been shown? Ask the referees who know him or her well.

- Describe several work situations that require high motivation and ask the applicant how he or she would react.

LOOK FOR THE MICHELANGELO MOTIVE

Perhaps the most impressive work of the Italian painter Michelangelo is the ceiling of the Sistine Chapel in Rome, a surface of some 6000 square feet. Once, while painting its frescoes, he was lying on his back on a high scaffold, carefully outlining a figure in the corner of the ceiling. A friend asked him why he took such pains with a figure that would be many feet from the viewer.

'After all,' said the friend, 'who will know whether it is perfect or not?'

'I will,' said the artist.

How would you define in a phrase that sort of inner

motivation? I cannot do so. Therefore I have called it simply the *Michelangelo motive*. I suggest you look for it when you are selecting people in future. Your team, company or organization needs it. Like Gideon in the story above, however, you may find that only one in every hundred applicants has the Michelangelo motive – but those few may be worth more to you than a great number of others.

THE CASE OF THE VITAL PETROL CAP

'What went wrong there was partly pilot error and partly a fault in the instrument display, which was unnecessarily complicated,' the senior licensing officer of the Civil Airline Authority told me. We were discussing an accident involving an aircraft. 'In this case the pilot had not completed all the Standing Operational Procedures before takeoff.' Himself an experienced pilot, he added: 'Of course I can't look out of the window to see if the engineer has screwed on the petrol caps.'

In my mind's eye I saw the engineer high above the ground on a dark wet night checking those caps. Our lives depend on his Michelangelo motive.

You may recall that Herzberg identified *the work itself* as a key motivator, one capable of giving long-lasting satisfaction. If Herzberg's conclusion is accurate, and if McGregor and others are right to suggest that creativity is much more widely distributed than was once assumed, then you will find the Michelangelo motive in many people in every field of work. Here are some of the signs to look for.

- a sense of pride in one's own workmanship
- an attention to the fine detail
- a willingness to stay longer or go to greater lengths in order to get the work right
- a total lack of the 'it's good enough, let it go' mentality
- an inner direction or responsibility for the work itself that dispenses with the need for supervision
- the ability to assess or evaluate one's own work, to be relatively independent of the views of others

In applying the Michelangelo principle or motive in your own life, beware of perfectionism – the disposition to regard anything short of perfection as unacceptable. Sometimes the best is the enemy of the good. Excellence may be within your grasp, but perfection eludes us humans. It is salutary to remember the story of the young man who spent many years searching for the perfect woman to make his wife. Eventually, after many heartbreaks, he met her – only to find that she was searching for the perfect husband!

GOOD AMBITION

'All competent men should have some ambition, for ambition is like the temper in steel. If there's too much the product is brittle, if there's too little the steel is soft; and without a certain amount of hardness a man cannot achieve what he sets out to do.'

Dwight Eisenhower

A business totally staffed with such people would probably founder! But without them a business is lost. You need a balance of motivation in a creative and innovative organization. In this context, what is important is that you should be able to select those who already have the Michelangelo motive for the jobs where that is a prime necessity. And I don't simply have people like engineers, architects, orthopaedic surgeons, civil airline pilots and dentists in mind. What work today doesn't require that motive and that integrity?

THE FEEDBACK THAT MATTERS

At her eightieth birthday celebration the internationally famous weaver Theo Moorman had words to say that apply to our lives as well as to our work:

'Set your sights high, otherwise the whole momentum collapses. Cherish your integrity and judgement. You can't work with one eye on the market, you have to stand for yourself. When I take my work off the loom, occasionally there's a comeback feeling in one's gut that tells one it is good. It's a feeling to be prized above rubies.'

CHECKLIST: SELECT PEOPLE WHO ARE ALREADY MOTIVATED

	Yes	No
Do you have people who are underperforming basically because they lack motivation?	❑	❑
Have you reviewed your selection procedures for *all* members of the organizational team within the last twelve months?	❑	❑

CHECKLIST: SELECT PEOPLE WHO ARE
ALREADY MOTIVATED (Cont)

	Yes	No
Do you now have ways other than the one-to-one interview for assessing:		
motivation	☐	☐
ability	☐	☐
personality	☐	☐

List three methods by which you can tell if someone has the Michelangelo Motive:

....

....

....

	Yes	No
Has any customer commented personally to you about the high motivation of any member of your staff within the last month?	☐	☐
Have you a clear idea of the annual costs that your organization has incurred by people leaving within six months of appointment *for any reason whatsoever*?	☐	☐

KEY POINTS

- 'Don't beat the pig to try and make it sing. It wears you out and annoys the pig. Much better to sell the pig for bacon and buy a canary.' In other words, you've got to have the right talent to begin with. It's no good trying to motivate somebody if they're wrong for the job.

- Usually motivation goes hand in hand with ability. People are good at what they love doing; they tend to love what they excel at. So that's your first indicator – do they enjoy their work? 'To business that we love we rise betime, And go to it with delight,' wrote Shakespeare.
- Remember that each team member matters. The principle of selecting those who are already motivated applies to everyone in the organization, not simply to managers or those who have a direct interface with the customer.
- You are looking always for three elements or dimensions in a person's work: motivation, ability and personality. For energy, competence and chemistry are all essential in any member of a high-performance team or organization.
- By analyzing your mistakes or errors of judgement and by reflecting upon the principles in this chapter you can develop your judgement (and interviewing skills) so that you select the best – and send away the rest.
- The presence of the Michelangelo motive in all your team will largely solve your problem of managing people who work at a distance from you. As that situation becomes more common, so the Michelangelo motive becomes more important.

No man will find the best way to do a thing unless he loves to do that thing.

Japanese proverb

14

SET CHALLENGING BUT REALISTIC TARGETS

> I wanna be the leader
> I wanna be the leader
> Can I be the leader?
> Can I? I Can?
> Promise? Promise?
> Yippee, I'm the leader
> I'm the leader
> OK what shall we do?
>
> Michael Rosen

As a leader you should both ask that question and see that it gets answered. The answers relate to the common TASK circle. What are we to do here? How are we going to do it?

In Part One I suggested that each of the three circles creates a magnetic field of motivation. If you come within its ambit you will feel its influence. The INDIVIDUAL self-evidently creates such a field, stemming from his or her needs. *Needs*, you recall, is a general term to cover anything which causes you to feel a lack or want. It may be food, security or company that you crave. Or information or knowledge. Or a better job. Or recognition. And so on.

EXERCISES

If a foreign visitor stops you in the streets of your home town and asks for directions, do you tend to give them?

Why do you think the Good Samaritan helped the mugged wayfarer?

Would you do the same?

When we come into the magnetic field of an individual in 'need, want or any other kind of necessity' we are drawn to help. We may block out the signals, often for good reason, but we will feel them. Sometimes, depending on our perception of what the other person wants, we may either hinder that person or act indifferently. In brief, I believe that all tasks are like stars that emit radio signals. We pick up these emissions, however faint, over our largely subliminal frequency band. If these signals include both CHALLENGING and REALISTIC goals they will tend to activate the motivational cells within us.

DEFINE YOUR STRATEGIC AIMS

It follows that one of your core skills as a leader will be to carve out parts of the common TASK that are finite. As the proverb says, 'You can only eat an elephant one mouthful at a time.' These more limited jobs become your TARGETS or OBJECTIVES. As an intermediary step, it's worthwhile to break down the TASK or PURPOSE into AIMS. For these AIMS or AREAS OF PURPOSE can then become the quarries in which you and your colleagues will shape your TARGETS or OBJECTIVES.

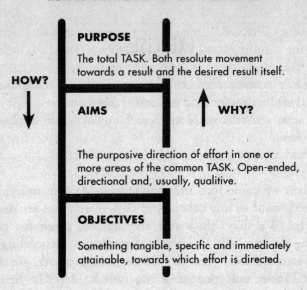

HOW? ↓

PURPOSE

The total TASK. Both resolute movement towards a result and the desired result itself.

AIMS   ↑ **WHY?**

The purposive direction of effort in one or more areas of the common TASK. Open-ended, directional and, usually, qualitive.

OBJECTIVES

Something tangible, specific and immediately attainable, towards which effort is directed.

Figure 14.1. The Jacob's Ladder Model

As you can see, PURPOSE, AIMS and OBJECTIVES should always relate to each other. Coming *down* the Jacob's Ladder answers the question *How?* How are we going to achieve the task? Answer: by breaking it down into these four or five areas of purpose or aims. How are we going to achieve any one of those aims? By breaking it down into tangible, specific and time-bounded objectives. These may be short-term or long-term. We often use the word *goal* for longer-term and difficult-to-attain objectives.

Coming *up* the Jacob's Ladder – *Why* are we tackling this objective? Answer: in order to achieve this aim. Why are we trying to accomplish that? In order to fulfil our task or purpose.

You may notice that I haven't included in the model

above the TARGET, which comes from an old German word for a light round shield and thence anything resembling it in shape, such as a mark to shoot at. It's useful here because it encompasses both the longer-term and shorter-term *objectives*. Your *target* is a result aimed at something to be attained, be it close at hand or far away – like landing a space probe on a distant planet by the year 2000. Coming back to earth – how do *you* effectively target a team or organization?

> Check: Is it specific?
> Is it clear?
> Is it time-bounded?

Now take a fresh look at your personal or team OBJEC-TIVES. First, ask yourself if they are REALISTIC in the sense that they fall within the bounds of feasibility. You may want to conduct the Boston Symphony Orchestra playing Beethoven's Fifth, but is that realistic when you consider your musical talent and what you have done with your life so far?

Secondly, is it a CHALLENGING target? Now challenge is a subjective matter. What challenges one person may daunt another. Do *you* perceive it as a challenge? Can you communicate it to the team so that *they* also perceive it that way? A challenge is an invitation or summons (ultimately from the TASK circle's magnetic field) to *a demanding or difficult task*. By its very nature it is one that will surely test your abilities. Your powers and resources may be stretched to their full extent. Often threatening, provocative, stimulating or inciting, a challenge is above all motivating.

'There is no inspiration in the ideals of plenty and stability,' wrote John Lancaster Spalding. People are capable of transcending self in the pursuit of high and demanding ideals.

Most people reveal this capacity in the way they respond better to a challenge. As I have said, there is a fine balance here. If objectives are totally unrealistic they will not appeal to people; if they are too easy to attain, on the other hand, they are also uninspiring. As a leader you have to get the balance right.

In the 3M Company, for example, managers are *challenged* by demanding goals. For instance, says Lewis W. Lehr, the former Chairman of 3M, in the field of innovation the targets are set to stretch all concerned:

> 'Our divisions shoot for a high target: In any given year, twenty five per cent of sales should come from products introduced within the last five years. Of course, not every division hits its target every year. But our managers are judged not only on their ability to make existing product lines grow but also on their knack for bringing innovative new products to market. So they have a built-in incentive to keep R&D strong.'

IT'S IMPORTANT TO AGREE OBJECTIVES

One certain litmus test of motivation is to look at the targets or goals that individuals or teams set themselves. The better an individual or group are, the more they will gravitate towards the REALISTIC-CHALLENGING end of the endeavour spectrum.

Should you always agree objectives? Bear in mind that people often initially dislike activities – such as learning to play a musical instrument – that later they find rewarding. Research has shown, as we have seen, that such is the case with tasks. Therefore, on one hand it is unwise for you as a leader to give the team or an individual in your team a totally free hand in setting targets. On the other hand, however, the principle is true that the more we *share* on decisions which affect our working lives, the more we are motivated to carry them out (see Figure 9.3 above, p. 115). If the person *accepts* that the objective is both realistic and desirable or important, then he or she will start drawing upon *their* 50 per cent of the motivational equation.

In the taking of a decision about a target there is a continuum of involvement, ranging from being told what to do at one end to full participation at the other. In *Effective Leadership* (1989) I have discussed this model of a continuum and the factors that you have to take into account if you are going to be perceived as a consistent yet flexible decision-maker.

These factors include, for example, such considerations as the ability, experience and maturity of those involved in the decision and its implementation, and the urgency within the time frame in which the decision has to be taken. Life-and-death issues may also be involved. Yet in order to gain *commitment* it is necessary to go as far towards participation as you can, subject to the limits which task, time and circumstance impose upon you.

Commitment, you may recall, is what happens when motivation becomes conscious and passes through the gates of decision on its road to action. People will always work best if they have had a hand in setting or agreeing on their targets. 'I have always worked hardest and best at self-imposed tasks,' said the poet and author Kathleen Raine. Isn't that true of yourself?

HOW TO MAKE THE EASY INTO THE DIFFICULT

In the 1970s John Curry, then world ice-skating champion, set himself the task of devising the first world-class ice-dancing shows. This is what he has to say:

'There were many things which at first sight looked impossible to translate from dancing to skating. But I do not believe in can't. I would not settle for doing a double jump instead of a triple. For if you start saying you can't do a particular thing, pretty soon the things that were easy become difficult.'

Artists and sportsmen of all kinds find great motivation in self-imposed targets that are realistic but challenging. If it isn't difficult, why do it? They are 100 per cent committed because they were 100 per cent party to the decision to attempt that task in the first instance.

Here lies the principle behind what used to be called Management by Objectives. If you tell people what to do they will probably do it – for money or from fear of dismissal. But if you wish to draw the best out of them engage their hearts and minds by winning assent – genuine agreement – to the realistic and challenging targets you propose or have in mind. Sometimes the team or individual concerned may surprise you by suggesting something even more demanding than your tentative goal. If it's still within the bounds of feasibility and if it doesn't detract from the broader efforts of the organization, why not say, 'Yes, let's have a go. Perhaps together and with a bit of luck we can pull it off.'

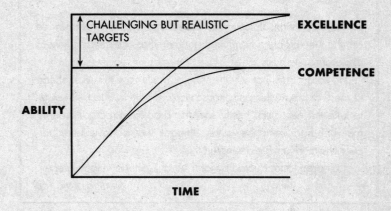

Figure 14.2 The Leadership Difference

You will notice that I have called it the leadership difference. Leaders make you partners in battle. And there are many sorts of campaign. Banesh Hoffman, who began his long collaboration with Einstein in 1937, once commented, 'If you worked with him he made you aware of a common enemy – the problem. But you become his partner in battle.'

Remember that if people look at the whole task before them, if it is truly challenging, they may well feel like returning to their tents. Your job as a leader is to break it down into *attainable* steps and focus the team's attention on the next step or phase in the chain of events that will lead to the desired result.

ONE STEP AT A TIME

Sir Henry Morton Stanley was asked if he had been frightened of the incredible, horrifying jungle that daunted previous explorers.

He said, 'I did not see the whole. I only saw this rock ahead of me; I only saw this poisonous snake which I had to kill in order to take the next step. I only saw the problem directly in front of me. If I had seen the whole thing I would have been too overwhelmed to have attempted this.'

George Lang, quoted by John Mack Carter and Joan Feeney.
Starting at the Top

As a management proverb puts it, 'An inch is a cinch, but a yard is hard.'

CHECKLIST: SET REALISTIC AND CHALLENGING TARGETS

	Yes	No
Are you clear about the *objectives* of your team now and for the next year?	☐	☐
Have you agreed or cleared them with:		
Your superior	☐	☐
Your team	☐	☐
Your colleagues	☐	☐
Do you see clearly how these targets relate to the *purpose* or mission of the organization, and one or more of its strategic *aims*?	☐	☐

Are the targets you have set the team or the
individual both *realistic* (i.e. feasible given
available time and resources) and *challenging*?   ❏   ❏

Good teams like to be stretched. Are you
challenging your team sufficiently?   ❏   ❏

Are all your targets related solely to short-term profit
(i.e. in the next quarter)? Give two examples of
targets achieved in the last year – both realistic and
challenging – which were *not* tied specifically to
short-term profit figures:

1 ....
2 ....

Do you take time and trouble to ensure that people
take the initiative in setting their own targets?   ❏   ❏

KEY POINTS

- The concept of task has built into it the element of
  difficulty or demandingness. If it was easy, it wouldn't be
  a task.

- Research into the psychology of being unemployed
  suggests that what people without jobs miss most are
  precisely the demands and disciplines imposed by a given,
  external task. A ship in harbour is safe, but that isn't what
  ships are for.

- So never be afraid to set realistic and challenging targets.
  People will be disappointed if you do not do so. As a
  leader you should guide people away from the easy tarmac

surfaces of mediocrity onto the runway from which you can take off together towards the stars.

- You won't do that unless you think clearly about the *purpose* and *aims* of your organization, and can break them down into more tangible, time-bounded and (if possible) measurable *targets*.

- '*It's a funny thing about life: if you refuse to accept anything but the best, you very often get it*,' said Somerset Maugham. Set your face against allowing people to perform below their level, producing second-rate goods or falling short of customer requirements. You serve them best by demanding that what needs to be done is done.

- Remember that organizations who have the hardest times are staffed by people who set the easiest targets! Only dead fish swim with the stream.

It is not enough to do our best. Sometimes we have to do what's required.

Winston Churchill

15

REMEMBER THAT PROGRESS MOTIVATES

We are motivated not simply by our individual needs but also by needs emanating from the common task. We WANT to finish what we are doing. The more significant the task, the stronger the need of the committed to complete it satisfactorily. John Wesley once spoke about 'the lust to finish'.

It is a sound principle that progress motivates. If people know that they are moving forwards it leads them to increase their efforts. We invest more in success.

Therefore it is important to ensure that people receive proper feedback. *Feedback* was originally a term in electronics meaning the return to the input of a part of the output of a machine, system or process. Without feedback people will not know if they are moving in the right direction at the right speed.

Conversely, feedback on relative lack of progress also motivates. For it concentrates minds on what must be done if success is yet to be achieved. If you confront people with the realities of their situation in this way, then the 'law of the situation' will do much of the work of motivation for you.

WHY FEEDBACK DOESN'T HAPPEN

Although the giving and receiving of feedback plays such a large part in improving both results and motivation it seldom happens effectively. Sometimes what purports to be feedback is no more than personal criticism. It is delivered thoughtlessly to express annoyance or anger, not to strengthen motivation and improve performance. More often people are given no accurate feedback on how they are doing or how they might be doing better. Many excuses are offered for this total omission:

- People *know* if they are doing a good job or not, so they don't need to be told.
- If you tell people they are doing well they will start taking it easy and become complacent.
- If you point out that things are not going well they will be unhappy and cause trouble.
- It's very difficult to do well and we lack the skills to do it.
- It's important but not urgent, and so we haven't time.
- As a personal development matter giving feedback is not relevant to the job in hand.

Such managers often imagine that other people are like clockwork toy cars, to be wound up at the beginning and then be left to run down. But we all need topping up. Giving information to people in the form of affirmative and constructive feedback maintains good performance. Above all, it encourages people to persevere; it keeps them moving confidently in the right direction despite difficulties or setbacks.

ENCOURAGING WITH POSITIVE FEEDBACK

Some time ago, I was facilitating a team event for a small management team of a financial organization in Scotland. On the final day it was decided to go clay pigeon shooting on a nearby estate to celebrate the success of the event and to cement the team building activity. I did not feel at all enthusiastic about this as I had never held a gun, let alone shot one. However, despite my trepidation and misgivings, it turned out to be a very positive experience.

When I reflected on why this was so I realized it was as a result of the way I had been treated by the instructor. Obviously he delivered some basic instruction as to how to use the gun safely, but it was what he did during the actual shooting that made the difference. After each shot, even if you had missed, he found some aspect of your approach to praise you about. Then, after you had reloaded and were preparing for the next shot he would give you one piece of advice about how you might improve. This approach raised my confidence and improved my shooting.

John Thatcher

Everyone succeeds at something. Catch people doing something right. Build on their strengths, small successes and steps forward. Giving your team as a whole, or an individual who reports to you, a colleague or even your superior some *affirmative feedback* (or praise) is just as important as giving them *development feedback* – constructive suggestions designed to improve performance in the future. The importance of such positive feedback will become even more clear in the next chapter, which is largely devoted to it. But at the end of the day it doesn't matter what you call it as long as you do it.

Paradoxically, in some ways it is even more difficult to give praise with skill than it is to give criticism. For praise can easily be perceived or misinterpreted as:

- patronizing
- insincere
- over-generous
- unspontaneous
- superior
- grudging
- calculated for effect
- unfair
- inaccurate
- condescending

Praise is a form of valuing. The word *praise* comes from the Latin for *price*. Thus praise is knowing and expressing the price or worth of what you see. It can refer to overall approval or – as in this context – to a specific accomplishment. Accuracy of judgement and honesty or integrity are essential, otherwise – at its worst – praise degenerates into the mere paying of empty and insincere compliments. Pleasant though such sounds may be providing you don't inhale – they have no motivational effects whatsoever.

THE ART OF INSPIRING WHILE INFORMING

Apart from your own professional competence and personal example there is probably no more effective means available to you for increasing the motivational bank balance than by talking to the assembled team about the tasks that lie ahead. At such meetings you can win them over to your way of thinking, providing you are manifestly making good sense with your plan of action. The art is to combine some inspiration with this work of giving information and receiving it. Inspiration is the descant that rises above information.

In fact, all communication – like these initial briefings – should be seen as opportunities of touching the hearts as well as the minds of others. If things are going reasonably well, you can make some incremental payments into the motivational bank account. Or you can prod, energize or enthuse if spirits are beginning to droop.

The golden rule, however, is *always to give information first before you attempt to encourage.* For inspiration always starts from knowing the realities of your situation. It is truth that inspires, never you.

Remember that you cannot make these necessary motivating interventions unless you are taking the heliview and observing closely what is going on. Watch the faces of those who work with you, for they will tell you more than words when people need some encouragement.

HOW TO MAINTAIN HIGH MORALE

Imagine that motivation in an organization, team or individual is rather like a bank balance. No one has an unlimited stock. When it is used up the effective effort collapses. The motivation in this sense is like capital. It is always being spent. The call on the bank may be only the daily drip-drip drain of seemingly endless problems and frustrations. Or it may be a sudden draft which threatens to close the account. Some major setback or disappointment, accompanied perhaps by the loss of the support of some stauncher spirit on whom the group has come to depend, can cause a catastrophic fall in morale.

You are enthusiastic and highly motivated yourself. As far as it lies within your power you have selected team members who are highly motivated. You have set or agreed realistic and challenging targets. Mission accomplished? Not at all — it's only just beginning. For motivation is not like something carved out of stone. It is more like bread in that it has to be continually made and remade. This is the key reason why you should always keep a close eye on the level of motivation or morale in individuals, team and organization. Morale covers both attitude and purpose or energy. It means:

- the mental and emotional attitudes of an individual or team to the functions or tasks assigned
- a sense of common purpose with respect to a group.

Now morale in the double sense of individual psychological well-being and *esprit de corps* can fluctuate very considerably. The two essential pillars of morale — a sense of purpose and confidence in the future — can be shaken if not shattered by the tremors and earthquakes of change.

The first question to ask yourself is how general is the loss of motivation and lowering of morale? Does it affect the whole team (or organization) or is it located in one or two individuals?

If the motivation or morale problem is general — a symptom or set of symptoms in the TEAM circle — the causes are almost always to be found in the TASK area. The symptoms might include the look or feel of the group — what you could call its *atmosphere*. How people talk both expresses or creates a certain atmosphere or climate. It may not be to your liking. Here are some indicative remarks:

'We are on a losing streak – we can never overtake the opposition now.'
'I don't see what good we are doing with all this extra effort.'
'Nobody seems to know where we are heading – we are going round in circles.'
'There's no future in this industry.'
'Why bother? We are beaten before we start.'
'If only we had a better leader.'
'The strategic plan is just a paper exercise to keep head office happy.'
'We are a second-class outfit in a global market – we don't have a hope of winning.'

Basically these sorts of remarks – usually heard in informal settings – signal dangers in the TASK circle:

- a lack of confidence in ultimate success
- a lack of confidence in present plans
- a lack of confidence in the leadership
- a lack of self-confidence and pride.

EXERCISE

You have recently been appointed manager of the Boulevard Hotel in your capital city. The Boulevard chain of holiday hotels is struggling to survive and a lot depends on whether or not you can turn this key hotel from being a loss maker into a profitable enterprise. After much heart-searching the Board have allocated a large sum from their diminishing reserve fund to renovate the hotel and upgrade its two restaurants.

'The real problem is the staff,' the President tells you. 'They are very experienced and well qualified but they have lost all confidence in themselves. They arrive late and leave early. They complain all the time, even to the customers. One waiter recommended a friend of mine stay at the Excelsior, our biggest rival! When you walk round the place you'll see what I mean. No one smiles. They are sullen and uncooperative. I can't make it out. Should we sack the lot? We pay them the going rates. But still everyone does as little as they can, the lazy bastards.'

Having arrived today you have summoned a meeting of all the staff in the ballroom tomorrow morning. What will you say to them?

Before you attempt to encourage or inspire your team or an individual see if you can give them some new *information* – some good news – in the area to the task. It may be some change or alteration in the plan that promises a higher probability of success, or that new resources – material or human – are now available or coming soon to help move things forward. Go back to the TASK circle in your own thinking and check out:

- the worth – or value of the overall end to all concerned
- the clarity of the common purpose or mission
- communication of the *why* as well as *what* and *how*
- the breakdown of aims into objectives
- the availability of the necessary tools and resources
- the quality of team leadership
- the level of participation or involvement in planning
- the soundness of the present plan
- what factors, if any, have been overlooked

If distortions and blockages in the TASK circle can be removed then the rivers and streams of team and individual energies should flow freely once more. So communicate the changes of direction and plan – the decisions taken to put the show on the road again. As you do so you will not only be inspiring confidence in the future but also engendering confidence in your leadership.

Doubtless the way ahead which you foresee for the team or organization will not be an easy one. Most roads of leadership go uphill. But people, especially if they have been fed with lies, false promises, specious hopes and empty visions, will welcome the plain hard truth. Your message is that the going will get more difficult. But if we work together and are determined success will be our reward.

THE WAY AHEAD

Our prospects never looked brighter, and the problems never looked tougher. Anyone who isn't stirred by both of those statements is too tired to be of much use to us in the days ahead.

John Gardner in *No Easy Victories*

By your words and actions communicate to the team your confidence in them. Tell them you believe in them – as people and as professionals. With the plan you have developed and with the resources that are available they can transform their performance. That will help to release the greatness that is within those who work with you. It's the message they have been craving to hear. Already by replanning, by bringing fresh reserves of one kind or another, you have prepared the dry sticks of new hope. Now they await only the flame of your words delivered directly and with inner conviction. Do that – and you have relit the rocket engines.

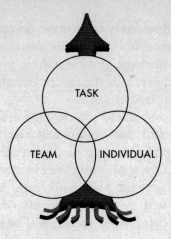

Figure 10.2   Give me fire and I will give you light

CHECKLIST: REMEMBER THAT PROGRESS MOTIVATES

	Yes	No
When work is in progress, do you actively encourage people?	❏	❏
Do you give people regular feedback on their progress, both as members of a team and as individuals?	❏	❏
Can you balance taking the heliview of the three circles with intervening effectively at critical points and then withdrawing?	❏	❏
Would you agree that good morale is an 'optional extra' in an organization?	❏	❏
Would you agree that good morale is an 'optional extra' in an organization?	❏	❏

Does the vision of your organization lift the spirits of its members? ❏ ❏

Do you believe that the production and selling of the goods and services that society needs is a basically uninspiring activity? ❏ ❏

Can you stimulate or spur on others to greater effort if progress slackens? ❏ ❏

Can you carry on working hard over long periods of time in difficult circumstances if no one encourages you? ❏ ❏

KEY POINTS

- Morale stems from the attitude an organization, team or individual holds to the common task. In a climate of high morale, people are eager to get to work. But morale, like the day's weather, can fluctuate.
- Courage is like a bank balance. If an individual overdraws on the account, he or she becomes anxious and stressed. Good leaders and good colleagues can do much to encourage or put new heart into those who become temporarily dispirited.
- More motivation is often better than more method. As a manager, take the heliview position and watch the interaction of the three circles as the action unfolds. You will then be able to see where to intervene with active help and words of encouragement.
- 'Those who are near will not hide their ability, and those who are distant will not grumble at their toil . . . That is

what is called being a leader and teacher of men.' So wrote Hsün-tzu, one of the Taoist school of thinkers in ancient China. The people may do it themselves – but you as leader can make a vital difference.

- Hope is the oxygen of the human spirit. Take another look at the corporate vision of your organization and its core values. How much hope is there on offer of a better future for humanity? Encouragement is more than verbal carrots or sticks, more than fine words: it should touch the spirit.

- Inspiration never travels alone. Use occasions when you are informing the team or individual of the situation, together with plans, developments or progress, to season your message with some encouragement. But remember that inspiration is best applied in drops to sore eyes, not in litres over people's heads.

'I believe the real difference between success and failure in an organization can very often be traced to the question of how well the organization brings out the great energies and talents of its people'.

Thomas J. Watson Jnr, former Chairman, IBM

16

TREAT EACH PERSON AS AN INDIVIDUAL

'What would you like next?' my host at the dinner table, a distinguished philosopher, asked me. 'May I eat fruit?' I asked, as he reached for the cheese and biscuits.

'No, no,' he replied, 'you can't do that, John.' I noticed a twinkle in his eye.

'But your wife has just kindly put a large bowl of fruit on the table . . .'

'Yes, yes, but you cannot eat *fruit* – you can eat an apple or a pear or a banana, but not *fruit*.'

In the context of this book the individual (or individuals) is equivalent to fruit, while the next person you meet known to you by name is an apple or a pear. Most books about managing people or – even worse – the 'human resource', give you what might be called *on-the-average* ideas about teams or individuals. You should always fine-tune them by entering into dialogue with those whom you know personally.

Unless you ask people what motivates them – what they want – you will not know. You cannot get that information out of any book (even this one) for most people haven't written a book about themselves. For we are all really individual fruits, not fruit in general. Even no two apples are alike. What motivates one person in the team may not motivate another.

Not that individuals will always be clear about what they want. Our motivation changes with age and circumstance. One of your functions as a leader may be to help individuals clarify what they are seeking at any given time in their careers.

In the context of the three-circles model, you should have a relation with the team as a whole *and* each individual member. These latter relationships – perhaps ten or twelve in number – will all be equal to you in value and in terms of the time you invest, but you may well find them very different in character. For a relationship is the chemical product of two people interacting, so none of your relationships will ever be duplicated.

FIRST TREAT EACH INDIVIDUAL AS A PERSON

Just to remind you, if you want to draw the best out of any individual you have to treat him or her as a person first and foremost – not as a man or woman, manager or worker, customer or supplier. Just as you may properly expect to be treated as a person in return. Nor can the moral obligation here be rephrased as 'You treat me as a person, and I'll treat you as a person'. For a moral person there is no such conditional clause. I *must* treat you as a person, whether you respond in kind or not, because you *are* a person. Therefore treating you as a thing – manipulating or using you in any way – will never work, at least in the long run.

These principles about all persons, rather than particular persons, strike me as important in the context of effective motivation and leadership for this reason. Your *attitudes* stem ultimately from what beliefs, perceptions or assumptions you hold about human nature. If you get your fundamental picture of man and woman wrong then a degree of falsity will eventually colour your derived attitudes to people at work.

Sense of trust	Trust towards oneself and towards others, as receiving and giving develops. Significant communication does not occur until some relationship of trust is established.
Sense of autonomy	A person needs to be able to assert his or her will and stand over against others as a separate person. He or she needs to be part of others and distinct from them, to belong and yet to be self-sufficient.
Sense of initiative	A person should be developing a sense of initiative. It is the power that moves people to begin things.
Sense of industry	Finding vocational work – work that has a fulfilling element – helps to develop a sense of industry. It plays a central part in personal life.
Sense of integrity	Integrity means first learning to adhere to standards or values outside oneself. This gives life reference points other than self-interest. It aids the development of wholeness.

| Sense of security | People like and need a sense of security which comes from understanding where they stand in relation to the other significant people in their lives. |

Figure 16.1   What to Foster in Persons

FINDING TIME FOR INDIVIDUALS

One of the problems that managers have is finding time for talking and listening to individuals *at all*, let alone in the context of finding out what motivates them. It is easy to neglect individual motivation in favour of meeting always and only with the team, especially if there is immense pressure in the task area.

'Once I have selected motivated people,' an international banker told me, 'then that's it. They know what the rewards are. They know, too, that we are in a tough business. If we don't perform, we shall all go down the drain. I lead from the front and I expect them to follow.'

'But don't you do anything more to encourage or motivate them?' I asked.

'John,' he replied, 'you have no idea of the time pressures we are under in this extremely competitive global market. "Keep the Best – Fire the Rest" is our motto. We don't pat people on the back or give them pep talks. We are results-driven. If they fail to contribute to the bottom line they are out.'

'It sounds very focussed on short-term results,' I commented.

'Precisely,' he replied.

Few things are more motivating to individuals than personal attention from you as their leader. You may be able to help people by coaching or counselling, so they develop as professionals and as leaders or managers. Such practical help is the best way of communicating the message to individuals in the team that *each of them matters to this enterprise*.

THE BEST LEADERS ALWAYS FIND TIME FOR THE INDIVIDUAL

General Sir Brian Horrocks commanded 13 Corps under Field Marshal Lord Montgomery (as he later became) at the battles of Alam Halfa and Alamein. In his autobiography he recalled how Montgomery found time even in the middle of a critical military campaign, to coach an individual member of his team.

'On the day after the battle [Alam Halfa] I was sitting in my headquarters purring with satisfaction. The battle had been won and I had not been mauled in the process. What could be better? Then in came a liaison officer from 8th Army headquarters bringing me a letter in Monty's even hand. This is what he said: "Dear Jorrocks,

Well done – but you must remember that you are now a corps commander and not a divisional commander . . ."

He went on to list four or five things which I had done wrong, mainly because I had interfered too much with the tasks of my subordinate commanders. The purring stopped abruptly. Perhaps I wasn't quite such a heaven-sent general after all. But the more I thought over the battle, the more I realized that Monty was right. So I rang him up and said, "Thank you very much."

I mention this because Montgomery was one of the few commanders who tried to train the people who worked under

---

THE BEST LEADERS ALWAYS FIND TIME
FOR THE INDIVIDUAL (Cont)

him. Who else, on the day after his first major victory, which had altered the whole complexion of the war in the Middle East, would have taken the trouble to write a letter like this in his own hand to one of his subordinate commanders?'

Some individuals may need coaching in this way; others may need a heart-to-heart talk on their prospects. All need encouragement. Most individuals, too, will admit to needing some prodding or goading to greater efforts from time to time. Knowing the most appropriate way to administer the spur in a given individual's case is a part of the art of leadership. One person may respond to a glance or a searching question, while another may need a more vigorous reminder.

In the Second World War the leader of Britain, Winston Churchill, was constantly stimulating his colleagues to greater efforts, as well as the nation by his inspiring speeches. Nobody who worked near him or within his reach had an easy time. 'I am certainly not one of those who need to be prodded,' he said. 'In fact, if anything, I am the prod.'

THE MISSING CASE OF THE LOW PERFORMER

'Where is it then?' said a manager who read this book at proof stage. 'Where is the case of the low performer? I can't see it below. I am especially interested in it because it's our biggest problem. We have done all we can to improve our selection systems. We communicate. We have incentive schemes. But still we have a number of low performers.'

Yes, even in a group of high achievers there will be between ten and fifteen who are truly outstanding, in the quality of their minds, willingness to take initiatives and ability to help and inspire colleagues. And you may have some six or seven at the other end of the spectrum who go 'off the boil' and become below average performers or even passengers.

'We've got rather more passengers than that', said my manager friend. 'Yes, we have some high flyers: the super-sales people, the production-target beaters, the workaholics who can be relied upon to do an excellent job. But they are only about 15 per cent of the people we employ. Have you anything I can do about the under-performers?'

Where is the case-study? There isn't one. For each of those working for you is an individual potential case-study. Ask people individually why they are not achieving their agreed targets. Find out what motivates them *now*. See if you can strengthen the overlap between their particular individual circles and the common task. Each of those low achievers is a case study in its own right. Go and talk to them – they have the answers to your questions. It is possible that you may both agree that they are in the wrong job.

RESTORING SELF-CONFIDENCE

'Man is tougher than iron, harder than stone, and more delicate than the rose,' declared a Turkish proverb. It neatly captures another paradox in human nature. Behind the toughest exterior there is often a vulnerable sensitivity, easily damaged by failures.

When have you been inspired? What were the ingredients in that experience? The example and enthusiasm of a teacher or leader. Yes, but what else?

> Malcolm Williams had become managing director at the early age of thirty of a small company making food-processing machinery. All went well until he fell out with the owning family on business strategy. 'We don't believe you can achieve those sorts of results,' they informed him. It soon became clear that two key members of the family had lost all confidence in him as a leader and manager, and so he took the redundancy package on offer.
>
> After two years of job-seeking, he began working as a sales representative in a large conglomerate. Several months later he was invited to apply to become chief executive of one of its small companies in Africa. 'Malcolm, we know you have great potential as a business leader – here is your opportunity to show us and yourself.' Malcolm Williams left the Chairman's office feeling completely inspired. His confidence in himself began to flood back. He proved worthy of the trust and in course of time rose to be Chief Executive of a major public company.

There are all sorts of reasons why a person's or a group's self-esteem can go into decline. Perhaps it was never naturally very high in the first place. Perhaps it has been sapped by repeated failures, criticisms, frustrations and defeats. If you can take someone who tells you or themselves 'I can't do it' and convince them that they can, then you are inspiring them. It's not so much a matter of infusing your spirit into their spirit. It's more a matter of stirring up the spirit, the latent human resource within them. Challenge may do that in part. But it has to be matched by your confidence in them. There is nothing more creative or rewarding than helping an individual who has been written off by others to turn disaster into success. Seize those opportunities for creative leadership if they come to you.

Encouraging	• Giving hope, courage, confidence or spirit, often accompanied by active help • Spurring, inciting, urging • Stimulating a person by help or reward • Recommending, advising
Heartening	• Renewing someone's spirit, especially to the point of giving them fresh courage in pursuit of a course of action
Inspiring	• Infusing with confidence or resolution • Firing with enthusiasm • Influencing, moving, guiding • Animating with a noble or exalted feeling • Elevating the mind • Enlivening or inspiriting; putting new life into
Supporting	• Implies that without the help given the thing or person helped might founder or fail. The help given is necessary for survival and growth

Emboldening	• Giving someone confidence to undertake something. • Imparting boldness or courage to others
Stimulating	• Rousing to action or exertion by pricking or goading • Inciting to do something • Quickening an activity or process

Figure 16.1   The Spectrum of Encouragement

Why not budget some more time to spend with individuals *on their own* in the next six months? You may, for example, be able to use committed time by sharing a journey with them. Or invite them to join you for a drink or a bite of lunch.

Why? Because each individual matters, both as an end in himself or herself and as a valued means to the common end. As Sir John Harvey-Jones, former Chairman of ICI, has written:

'Management, above everything else, is about people. It is about the accomplishment of ends and aims by the efforts of groups of people working together. The people and *their individual hopes and skills* are the greatest variable and the most important one.'

CHECKLIST: TREAT EACH PERSON AS AN INDIVIDUAL

	Yes	No
Does your organization treat all individuals – of all ages, sexes and ethnic backgrounds – as persons?	❑	❑
Do you agree that each individual has an inalienable worth or dignity simply by virtue of being a person?	❑	❑
Do you know all the names of those on your team, and the members of their teams if they are leaders?	❑	❑
Can you identify the ways in which each individual reporting to you *differs* from all the others in personality, ability and motivation?	❑	❑
Do you accept the idea that people's motivation may change from time to time as their lives unfold?	❑	❑
Have you had set aside time to get to know and work with each individual member of the team?	❑	❑
Do you see the role of coach to each individual, as far as professional competence is concerned, as being a core part of your leadership responsibilities?	❑	❑
Do you feel that your organization responds to you as a unique individual and not just a manager? Has it shown flexibility when your home circumstances have changed?	❑	❑

KEY POINTS

- You cannot eat fruit, only apples or grapes and so on. The same principle applies to individuals.
- If you don't treat individuals as persons, there isn't much point in treating persons as individuals – for they won't respond.
- There isn't any other way but to talk to a person as an individual and to listen to what he or she says. Doing that is stimulating in itself, but it may also help you to understand and work with the natural grain of that person's motive energy.
- Individuals who fall by the wayside should merit your special attention. For they call for *creative* leadership, the most rewarding kind of all.

I am persuaded that every being has a part to play on earth: to be exact, his or her own part which resembles no other.
                                                                                      André Gide

17

PROVIDE FAIR REWARDS

All work implies this element of balancing what we give with what we expect to receive. Fairness or justice means that the return should be equivalent in value to the contribution. Performance ought to be linked to rewards, just as promotion should be related to merit. Ninety per cent of people ninety per cent of the time operate on this rational or 'expectancy-theory' model.

The former — getting financial rewards fair — is easier said than done in many work situations. But the principle is still important and ways of applying it have to be found. Justinian wrote that 'Justice is the constant and unceasing will to give everyone his right or due.' That genuine and sustained intention is expected from any leader who has discretion over the distribution of rewards.

The principle has to be applied with especial care over monetary remunerations, for if fairness is not *perceived* there it can breed a lack of motivation and low morale. When remuneration is poor, workers put less effort into their jobs. Money is a key incentive. Therefore proper job evaluation schemes, involving a representative group of work people in the judgements about the financial worth of jobs, is vitally important.

MONEY, MONEY, MONEY

A famous property developer was once asked what were the most important criteria for buying commercial property. 'Location, location, location,' he replied. When it comes to rewards for work done, it's tempting to reply in the same vein about money.

There are, of course, many rewards apart from money that we gain from working, as Maslow's hierarchy of needs illustrates. Opportunities for professional development and personal growth are especially valuable to good people. But money has a strategic importance for most people, not least as a measure of recognition for the significance of their contributions. As the means of exchange and as a store of wealth, money is probably the most useful material reward you can give.

The actual part or role that financial remuneration plays in a person's motivation will be subject to wide variations from individual to individual. For the value of money as a motivator will depend upon the individual's needs and expectations, as we saw in exploring 'expectancy theory' (Chapter Four). The strategic importance of money, however, stems from its unique set of functions or characteristics.

FUNCTION	NOTES
Means of Exchange	Money is now our principal means of exchange. This is its primary function. It is often eclipsed, however, by the next function described.

Store of Wealth	Storing or saving money is our most convenient way of stockpiling wealth. Wealth (or money in this sense) is purchasing power. Providing it isn't stolen or devalued by inflation, money in the bank is deferred purchasing power.
Basis for Comparison	Unlike most motivating agents money can be measured precisely. Therefore it is a yardstick or measure for comparison – with other people and other organizations. Salary or income increases also form one measure of individual career progress.
Means of Recognition	Money in the form of prizes, bonuses, or special awards can also be a powerful means of recognition or saying 'thank you'.
All-Embracing	Money can obviously be used to satisfy the more 'basic' needs – food, shelter, health and security. It can also play a part in meeting our 'higher' needs. Education, for example, may contribute to self-fulfilment but it has to be paid for. Travel likewise.

Figure 17.1 The Functions of Money

We have lost faith – perhaps temporarily – in the medieval doctrine (based on the laws of reciprocity and equivalent dealing) that there is a *just wage* for any piece of work. We accept that wages or salaries or fees – like prices – are determined in the market places where those services are hired. Fairness is a perception by a reasonable person that the remuneration offered falls within the band of the 'going rates' for the work in question. The band or scale is always under pressure from both parties: those who ask for more and those who want to give less.

In discussing the principle or law of reciprocity I suggested that if you give more you will tend to receive more. Does this apply to money? If you pay people 'over the odds' or beyond the accepted upper end of the market-rate-for-the-job pay band, will they transcend the normal limits of performance for your organization?

WHY SALARY CAN MAKE YOU UNHAPPY

'Since money accompanies increases in status, responsibility, success, independence, or security, money is the element that is measured and talked about, not the underlying factor. It has been frequently observed that we are more concerned about comparisons in our disfavour than we are pleased about comparisons in our favour. In other words, we use money as a comparative measuring stick. When *any* of the comparisons are unfavourable, inequitable, we are dissatisfied. When they are favourable we put it down to 'luck'. In a sense it is not money that is a hygiene factor, as Herzberg argues, but 'equity'. The absolute levels of pay are not often an issue but the equitable level, in relation to others, to one's own pay curve, to future expectations and self-concept. Many trades union arguments are about equity, not money as such'.

Charles Handy, in *Understanding Organization* (1993)

Personally I still accept Herzberg's insight that salary has more power to make you dissatisfied or unhappy than it has power to motivate you. Even the effects of a generous salary increase tend to wear off as you (and your expenditure) psychologically adjust to the new level of income. That's not an argument against paying people proper salaries. It does warn you, however, not to expect salary rises beyond a certain level to bring dramatic increases in motivation.

In summary, the case for paying people a proper salary is based upon justice or equity, not upon motivational considerations. If you pay less than what is perceived by reasonable people to be the fair rate, then you will probably generate dissatisfaction and possibly a decline in motivation. Good salary is a necessary cause for getting the best out of people, but it isn't a sufficient one – especially if it stands alone.

PERFORMANCE-RELATED PAY

At the other end of the spectrum from salary-workers and wage-workers are those who get paid by the piece of work or job they do. These include a whole variety of people – gardeners, authors, decorators, management consultants. Because the customer pays the worker directly after the job is done there is a stronger element of relating payment to performance.

What seems to work best with human nature is some mix or combination of the two methods of payment: fixed and variable.

Most individuals, certainly if they are bread-winners for young families, would like or prefer a *fixed* income.

Then you know you can pay the mortgage and the supermarket bills, buy the clothes and pay for essential utilities.

But we also like a *variable* income, which depends upon our own choice, efforts and skills. Earning this second kind of money is less predictable and more exciting. Perhaps it appeals to the hunter-gatherer instinct in us.

One night I was working under lights on the deck of an arctic trawler gutting fish. We had been working at it for almost sixteen hours, hauling in the trawl, releasing the silver fish in great cascades. A cold icy wind flecked with snow made the trawler roll.

'Good news, lads,' the mate announced. 'The skipper says we have just run into another big shoal of cod. We should have another three or four hours work tonight.'

'What bad luck,' I said to myself, feeling exhausted. For the last hour I had thought about nothing but my bunk in the warm foc's'l. 'What bad luck.'

'Come on now, Jack,' the mate said to me. 'Remember that I get a share of the catch and so do you. We shall make some real money on this trip.' And we did. Thanks to that run of cod my share of the catch and the extra codliver money we received as well almost doubled my wages as a deckhand learner for the three-week voyage.

The principle of fixed-variable income seems to work across a wide cross-section of professions and industries. Surgeons working for the National Health Service in Britain, for example, receive a salary but they also have negotiated contracts which allow them to earn fees from private patients. Taxi drivers and waiters have variable income in the form of tips, in principle performance-related. The popularity of overtime on the shopfloor is another instance of the principle at work.

A more ambitious extension of this principle is to make a part of someone's remuneration fixed (the traditional salary or wage) and part of it related to performance. A sales representative, for example, may receive commission over and above his salary on the sales he or she makes.

This principle does provide an important element in motivating others. From the story of the Arctic trawler you can see that it works. It gives people a share in the success of the common task. Apart from the financial rewards, people who are in some form of profit-sharing also tend to feel more motivated or committed. They have become partners in the enterprise. Nor is such a commitment confined to managers who (like the mate on my trawler) stand to make greater gains from the shares than the workers.

THE CASE OF THE DESPERATE OWNER

James Gilroy started up a company making a form of prefabricated, low-cost but high-quality housing. He had inherited from his father a family mansion, some 3000 acres of agricultural land and a large tax-bill. The house-building company was one idea for diversification.

All went well at first, but then recession and some adverse publicity hit the business hard. James struggled to motivate the work force, but to little avail.

Then one day he went down to the yard and called a meeting of the 18 remaining workers. He showed them all the accounts and the order book, explaining that they were approaching bankruptcy. He then offered 20 per cent of the profits to the workforce.

'That's what we have been waiting for,' said their natural leader.

In a year the company broke even and went on to make a good profit. When it was eventually sold for a handsome sum, everyone had profited from the venture.

Performance-related pay can take several forms. Giving a *bonus* is perhaps the most common one. A bonus, from the Latin for 'a good thing', is money or its equivalent given in addition to what is usually or strictly due as compensation. A bonus is over and above what is expected. In prospect its power to motivate can become diminished if a run of success leads people to expect the bonus more or less as part of their standard remuneration. The lessening or absence of a bonus can then create dissatisfaction.

Another issue arising out of performance-related pay is tying it down appropriately. Do you reward the whole organization for success with a corporate bonus, divided up in terms of rank? This was the principle employed in the Royal Navy in Nelson's day, when a captured prize ship was auctioned and the windfall profit shared out according to a scale based on rank. The captain obviously received the lion's share, but sailors in fortunate ships could become relatively wealthy. No wonder they wanted to serve in ships led by captains like Nelson!

Or, do you reward the team? But it's sometimes very difficult, even with the wonders of information technology, to allocate profit to a particular team in a large organization. Teamwork by all parts of an organization – not least finance, accountancy and administration – plays a part in the success of the 'profit-centres'. The same problem arises if you attempt to make part of an individual's salary or pay dependent upon performance.

These issues and questions do not, I hasten to add, invalidate the principle. But you do have to consider them carefully, especially if you are trying to introduce an element of performance-related pay into non-profit making organizations. If you get it wrong you may be deepening the latent divisiveness in all organizations, breaking up the team or frustrating individuals. Perhaps even more seriously, you may be propagating the assumption that personal gain-seeking is the principal motive in human nature and the one most appropriate in a service organization. Do you think that either of those propositions is true?

How do you avoid the pitfalls of applying the fixed-variable principle and still harvest the benefits? If you are leading an organization you may need to seek outside specialist help, if you haven't done so already. The principles are to keep any profit-sharing or performance-related element as simple as possible and to ensure that it is not perceived by any reasonable team member or employee as being unfair.

MOTIVATING BY INCENTIVES

Profit-sharing schemes, whether by giving people shares in the business or by distributing a result-based bonus, are the *strategic* way of relating performance to rewards in a fair way. They are certainly fair. They are also attractive from the employer's angle. If there are no profits then there is no bonus. If no one buys this book then the publisher doesn't have to pay me any royalties. On the other hand, if thousands buy your product or service then you share in the rewards.

Motivating by incentives is more *tactical* in nature. Staff motivation schemes can be very effective at getting employees to go the extra mile, so they merit discussion here. Similar schemes are often directed at consumers – such as stamps schemes or free air travel miles – but these belong more to the realm of sales promotion and therefore fall outside the scope of this book.

IN THE BEGINNING

In 1922 an assistant in a luggage store in Dayton, Ohio, named Elton F. MacDonald was approached by the sales manager of a local manufacturing corporation.

'Can you supply us with a number of briefcases which I can offer as prizes to our sales representatives in the company's forthcoming sales competition?' he asked.

MacDonald, who was only eighteen years old, soon concluded the sale. 'Don't you think it would be a good idea if you offered luggage or other goods as prizes in a follow-up contest to maintain momentum?' he suggested to the sales manager. After that second sale he devised a leaflet listing a number of prizes, varying in value, which winners could choose from, depending on the achievement level. From this acorn grew the world's first professional incentive company.

During the following decades the list of merchandise grew, culminating in incentive travel. Also those participating in incentive schemes widened beyond the sales force to include all managers and employees. It is now applied beyond the company to once-removed participants: wholesalers, distributors, dealers and retailers. The aim of such motivation-by-incentive schemes is simply to improve performance, such as:

- increasing sales
- improving after-sales customer service
- increasing product knowledge
- improving accuracy of form filling

Whatever the aims, research suggests that incentives schemes — if properly constructed and planned — can produce performance improvements of up to 25 per cent. Even so, putting in place an effective incentives scheme isn't easy. Correctly judging, for example, which of the various awards available is best suited to your staff can make all the difference between success and failure.

AWARD	FOR	AGAINST
Cash	Easy Cost-effective Flexible Most used by companies	May cause staff to think that managers are cold and calculating. Can be seen by staff as a manipulation of their time and skill. Can look an easy way out. Additional cash is frittered away on household expenses. Nothing to show for it. Many companies have bonus and profit-sharing schemes in place. Money is seen as employees' right.

AWARD	FOR	AGAINST (Cont)
Vouchers	Easy	Can be made to look more glamorous than cash.
Merchandise	Gives choice Suggested real effort on part of management	Greater administrative costs, as an awards brochure has to be printed.
Travel	Best motivator in terms of perceived value Appeals most to husbands or wives or partners of winners	Most expensive. High administrative costs. May create ever higher expectations for next year!

Figure 17.2   Incentive Awards

There is no point in having an incentives scheme unless it is well administered. The costs must be set against the probable benefits. You may believe that it is enough to motivate people – as far as material rewards go – simply by paying them a good salary with a bonus or profit-sharing element in it, and many leading companies do find that offering just that little bit extra in the form of prizes for competitions does make a difference. But make sure that people compete on fair terms and with equal opportunities for success. Also, don't over-emphasize competition: remember that it produces losers as well as winners, and losers can feel demotivated. If you go down this road make it fun and ensure that everyone keeps it in proportion.

CHECKLIST: PROVIDE FAIR REWARDS

	Yes	No
Do you think that the financial or financially related rewards system in your organization is perceived to be unfair?	❑	❑
Would you agree that money doesn't motivate you personally beyond a certain point?	❑	❑
Is your own financial reward made up of a *fixed* and a *variable* element?	❑	❑
Do you believe in performance-related pay?	❑	❑
Have you resolved in your organization the problems of whether the variable (performance-related) element should be paid to the organization, team or individual?	❑	❑
Would improvements in your information systems help you to introduce improvements in rewarding performance in the next year?	❑	❑
Have you considered in-centre schemes in areas other than for sales people?	❑	❑
Does your organization's compensation system adequately and accurately reward the behaviours that publicly it values?	❑	❑
Do senior managers ever award themselves pay rises, bonuses or share-options when they expect others to do without them?	❑	❑

KEY POINTS

- Money is the key element in rewarding work today because it is a means of exchange, store of wealth, basis for comparison, means of recognition and all-embracing in terms of our needs – and those of our families.
- Yet money still has more power to make you unhappy or dissatisfied in work than it does to make you highly motivated. Its motivational effects tend to wear off. Money remains an extrinsic factor, whereas the longer-lasting motivators are intrinsic in work itself. Both are desirable.
- Performance-related pay is sound in principle but difficult to apply in practice.
- As a general rule, people like to have a *fixed* element to their salaries and a *variable* element, which is more directly dependent on results.
- In keeping with that principle, incentive schemes have a part to play in a total motivational strategy. But they are more useful as methods of recognition, and cash is by no means always the best award. The costs of running such schemes always have to be balanced against their benefits.

You get more of the behaviour you reward. You don't get what you hope for, ask for, wish for or beg for. You get what you reward.

Michael le Boeuf

18

GIVE RECOGNITION

We all value positive recognition – that precious moment when someone important expresses some real appreciation for what we have contributed.

When we know that we have worked hard and have earned some recognition, don't we *want* it? If it is not forthcoming – from the team leader or colleagues in the team – we tend to feel unnoticed, unvalued and unrewarded. Our motivation drops, our energy level falls and our spirit droops.

Therefore don't underestimate the power of recognition as a motivator. It's the oxygen of the human spirit. If you turn back to Herzberg's research in Part One you will see how high people rate recognition as a factor in job satisfaction. For many people the prospect of recognition is more important than money as an incentive to great effort. As Milton wrote:

Fame is the spur that the clear spirit doth raise . . .
To scorn delights and live laborious days.

Where does recognition come from? It can have a variety of sources. In the case of a famous person it's a matter of public estimation. Fame comes from the Latin word *fama*, meaning *report*. So fame is how people talk about you, which adds up to your personal reputation. If you are much talked about (especially favourably) you will acquire a public reputation or renown. If that reputation is based upon significant achievements, then – congratulations – you are really famous.

Of course individuals can more easily achieve a kind of spurious fame by gaining the attention of many people for whatever reason. A footballer, television interviewer or pop star, for example, can easily become famous in our society. Although such fame still carries positive overtones, it can simply suggest popularity or general recognition rather than discriminating approval or inherent excellence. The media can to a large extent make or break this form of popularity or recognition. If you can afford to do so and are so minded you can even hire a public relations firm to get people to talk about you or your company in the way that you like.

The vast majority of us, however, are not destined to become famous in the real sense of the word. There has never been a time in history which has seen greater achievements than this present decade, but we tend now to achieve as members of teams.

> Yesterday I boarded an aircraft bound for Amsterdam at London Heathrow. As we waited in the queue for taking off I saw out of the window one of the Concordes being towed past, gleaming in the sunlight. What an achievement! But I could not think of the names of those who designed and made it. Can you?

It follows that for most of us recognition will be particular rather than general. It will come from those who know us personally or professionally. As a leader or team member – *give recognition*.

CHARACTERISTICS OF RECOGNITION

Recognition needs to come both formally and informally. There should be formal occasions when you recognize the quality or value of a particular contribution, be it an individual or team effort. There will also be plenty of informal opportunities for expressing appreciation as well. But recognition in both forms should have certain hallmarks or characteristics:

- Giving recognition should respect the basic leadership principle of treating everyone in a fair and equal way.
- It should reward real achievements or contributions to the common good, not self-seeking gains.
- It should reflect the core values of the organization.
- It should serve to guide and encourage all concerned.
- Where possible, therefore, it should be given in a public way in front of the working group or organization.
- Remember to give recognition informally as well as formally.
- Above all, it must be *genuine* and *sincere*, or – in a word – *real*.

That last point is crucial. People see through insincerity. Give appreciation when it is merited. But don't wait for obvious occasions to shout at you. Remember to take the leadership heliview as described in Chapter 9. Go out into the highways and byways of your organization and find legitimate reasons to compliment or thank people. Most of the time, if you keep your eyes and ears open, you will easily see actions, performance or results that deserve recognition. At other times you may have to look under the stones. For your world is full of things deserving attention and praise *that are not easy to see*.

Many people, for example, simply do what has to be done to accomplish the task, without seeking to draw any attention to themselves. Such people are modest in the sense that they are not aggressively self-assertive, or vain or presumptuous. They see their contributions as moderate or small in scale. If given recognition or reward they will genuinely accept it in an understated way, and not merely act as if they are doing so. The more unassuming and unpretentious you are the less you will wish or demand that others treat you in a special way or harbour illusions about your own importance. There is no display to attract your attention. Incidentally, as a leader you should yourself fall into that category.

THE TRUE GLORY

The great majority of leaders have been content to work in their chosen field without thought of honours or rewards; and the unacknowledged debt the world owes to them in all fields is enormous. In that connection I cannot do better than quote the words of Joseph Lister, the discoverer of antiseptic surgery and perhaps the greatest leader in medicine this country has produced.

When in 1898 he received the freedom of the city of Edinburgh he said: 'I must confess that highly, very highly as I esteem the honours which have been conferred upon me, I regard all worldly distinctions as nothing in comparison with the hope that I may have been the means of reducing in some degree the sum of human misery.'

Therefore if you cannot see outstanding achievements that deserve some recognition, keep looking. Don't reserve your appreciation and praise for achievements over and above the call of duty. Look for *levels of excellence* in the work that people are being paid to do. In every job there is a difference between average or normal performance and excellence. And that applies to the more routine or administrative jobs in your organization: the ones that serve the day-to-day *maintenance* needs of the organization rather than its more future-oriented work.

Sally Bromptom worked in the accounts department of a medium-sized printing company called Denny and Jenkins Ltd. Her promptness in sending invoices, her accuracy and her unfailing courtesy over the telephone impressed one major customer so much that he commented when he met the managing director at a trade fair. 'We like dealing with you,' he said, 'partly because your financial transactions with us are so businesslike and friendly.' 'Thank you,' said David Smith, the managing director, 'we like to please our customers.' But he neglected to find out who in accounts handled this particular customer's account. In consequence, Sally received no recognition from him at the time. But a little later . . .

Yes, such quality work is *expected* in return for salary or wages. No doubt Sally Bromptom in the story regarded the service she provided as 'part of the job'. Yet if you don't thank occasionally your team members for doing routine tasks consistently well, they will probably feel rather taken for granted. Think of the routine tasks you do at home. Doesn't it refresh your spirit if someone at some time expresses some appreciation for the meal on the table, a clean house, washed clothes, a garden in good order, being collected or delivered in the car? Notice that we do not look for recognition all the time – just once in a while is enough.

Even without outstanding attributes or contributions on any noticeable scale each member of the team deserves praise just for being an effective member. In motivation the secret is to treat each person as an individual. For each of us has our own particular fuse, and what motivates one individual may not motivate another. But there is a prior law that you should treat *every individual as a person*. To be a person is to have dignity or worth, both in who you are in yourself and in what you contribute to others – the rent you pay for your place on earth. When you praise an individual as a valued member of the team you are affirming their value as a person. We do not work for bread alone. Sometimes, not every day but just sometimes, thank the team or an individual member for coming to work.

EXERCISE

Make a list of all those in your organization who normally receive little attention and no commendation. They include the people who keep the whole system running smoothly. Let me start you off.

1. receptionist   6.
2. telephone operator 7.
3. security guard   8.
4. typist   9.
5.   10.

You can extend your list to include such people working in organizations that impinge on yours, such as suppliers, retailers or customers, with whom you come into contact. Giving feedback to the appropriate manager in them about excellent service helps both that organization to give praise and also cements your friendship with it. Perhaps a good customer is one who gives back recognition as well as justified complaint, not just money for the goods or services.

THE FIRST STEP

There are skills involved in giving recognition as there are in fulfilling all the functions of leadership (as opposed to merely performing them in a perfunctory way). We have touched upon some of the basic elements in the art of praising others. It is proverbially both rewarding and difficult to do really well.

PRAISE AND BLAME: SOME PROVERBS

An honest person is hurt by praise unjustly bestowed.
Too much praise is a burden.
I praise loudly, I blame softly.
Our praises are our wages.
The most pleasing of all sounds – that of your own praise.
Be sparing in praise and more so in blaming.
Praise is always pleasant.
Praise makes good people better and bad people worse.

Don't imagine that because giving recognition requires skill that means it is necessarily calculated, lacking in spontaneity or even manipulative. Art and skill are not opposed to being natural or spontaneous. They help you to be your best or natural self in an effective way. 'Grace does not destroy nature', wrote Thomas Aquinas, 'but perfects it.'

Also remember that by *skills* I include very basic things. Consider this second episode in the story of Sally Bromptom.

At a meeting of all the staff at Denny and Jenkins Ltd, called to introduce a new total quality management programme, the managing director David Smith suddenly remembered what that major customer had said about the accounts department.

'I want to congratulate you all,' he said. 'But especially . . .' He looked down at his file. 'One person in particular . . .' he began again. '*What is his name?*' he whispered to the finance director, who whispered the same question to the accounts manager.

'They don't even know my name,' said Sally to her

neighbour. She found the public thank you that followed rather embarrassing. It could not eclipse the realization that she was a nameless person, even to the finance director, in a company that employed 250 people.

To recognize means literally to know again. You recognize at a meeting an acquaintance as previously known. Recognition in this sense of knowing again usually involves recollecting some distinctive feature. Hence the extension of the word recognition to perceiving clearly and acknowledging worth with appreciation. If you do not recognize someone in the primary sense – as a person you know by name – how can you recognize them in the second sense of appreciating their value?

Therefore your first step as a leader is to learn the names of your team. That will not be difficult if you are a *team leader* (the accounts section manager). It becomes more so if you are an *operational leader*, with a number of teams reporting to you. A *strategic leader*, heading up an organization, may find the precept of knowing everyone's names almost impossible to follow. Is it? At least you should know the names of every manager.

Long ago Xenophon, the Greek general who as a young man was a student with Socrates, stressed the importance for a military leader of knowing the names of his officers. His ideal general made a special study of them

'for he thought it passing strange that, whilst every mechanic knows the names of the tools of his trade and the physician knows the names of all the instruments he uses, the general should be so foolish as not to know the names of the officers under him.'

Xenophon pointed out that those who are conscious of being personally known by their general do more good than any others.

Even when the Grand Army of France numbered over half a million men Napoleon still knew the names of the officers in all the regiments, so that when he visited a regiment he could address the officers by name. Such was his extraordinary power of memory that he also knew the places where the regiments were recruited and had gained distinction. No other general in history, with the possible exceptions of Alexander the Great or Julius Caesar, has better understood and applied the *power of recognition* as a motivator of people than Napoleon. It must be added that he often used it in a cynical and manipulative way, as a means to achieving his own vaunting and self-centred ambitions.

HOW TO RECOGNIZE PERFORMANCE

Like most armies since the days of the Greeks and Romans, Napoleon could offer an array of titles, honours, promotions and medals as tokens of recognition. Such honours systems have an important part to play in giving recognition but they are not the whole story.

Money can sometimes be used as an expression of appreciation, but it has relatively little value in this context (see Incentives, p. 219). It can create an expectation that good work – or even routine work well done – will be rewarded with money. Gifts of money can also establish precedents. Because money is a universal measure, financial rewards between teams or individuals can more easily be compared. If, by comparison, the monetary gift is perceived to be unfair then it will breed dissatisfaction – the reverse of your original intention.

A possible exception to the principle of not using cash in this way is provided by suggestion schemes aimed at saving money. When staff make suggestions for changes in work that produce direct savings, it makes sense to pass on some of these savings to those responsible for the ideas. Suggestion schemes, however, are like incentive schemes in that they have to be properly designed, managed and maintained.

The primary way of giving recognition is in words of thanks, especially in front of peers. Other tokens or gifts can be used to support them. A letter of commendation is also often greatly valued. Make sure that a copy goes into the person's file – the equivalent to being 'mentioned in despatches'.

When he was Chairman of ICI John Harvey-Jones used to send out about a hundred crates of wine each Christmas to outstanding performers, together with a handwritten note of appreciation. Where appropriate he also thanked the wives of those managers among them who had been overseas a great deal and thus away from home.

On a course of diocesan bishops and their staffs at St. George's House in Windsor Castle I told this story. Most of the bishops dismissed it on the grounds that the Church couldn't afford boxes of wine.

But one bishop went home and found a retired priest, now bedridden, and asked him to look through all the 500 parish magazines for stories of faithful service, such as a choir member retiring after many years in some small parish. The bishop then penned a personal note of appreciation. Some months later I stayed with a friend in that diocese and I met one recipient of the bishop's postcards – an organist who had completed thirty years service. 'It was lovely to get his letter,' he said, 'just like receiving a crate of wine!'

There are plenty of ways of reinforcing your words of thanks. Here are some ideas:

- a day off with pay
- a small dinner party
- tickets for theatre, concert or sports event
- some small gift, such as a pen
- a special assignment of interest and importance
- a job title change, promotion or new position

The list doesn't end there. Think creatively. Seek out new and attractive ways to show that you value the contributions of those who make it possible for the team to achieve its realistic and challenging targets. The culture of your organization will doubtless have precedents for recognizing and rewarding outstanding performance, but there is no reason why you shouldn't develop that tradition. Ask the team for ideas.

BE SPARING IN PRAISE

Lastly, a word of caution. Don't overdo it. People will be immensely pleased (at least inside) if you give them appreciation. If they deserve recognition for something out of the ordinary, they should be given it. The laws of reciprocity and equivalence will be at work, so people half-expect a matching or equivalent reward in the form of the esteem of others, if nothing else. In fact there are few things more valuable to us than the love of others. That is perhaps why the Roman Emperor and philosopher Marcus Aurelius counselled leaders: 'Love those people heartily that it is your fortune to be engaged with.'

But words of praise and appreciation, like money, can be devalued if they are multiplied and used without thought. For want of care or accuracy in language managers end up using superlatives all the time for effect. Such inflated language, worse than understatement, loses its cutting edge. Does a good word from you have real value? It won't do so if you throw your pearls around as if they were dried peas.

EFFECTIVE PRAISE

Stern-faced symphony conductor Otto Klemperer expected the best from his players and didn't go into raptures when he got it. After one performance, however, he was so pleased with the orchestra that he could not repress saying, 'Good!' Overwhelmed, the musicians burst into applause.

'Not *that* good,' grumbled Klemperer, reverting to character.

Be sparing in praise, but be liberal with thanks.

SEIZE EVERY OPPORTUNITY

Despite all that is written about money I believe that recognition is often an even more powerful motivator. As I hinted, money anyway often means more to people as a tangible symbol of recognition than as the wherewithal to buy more material goods. This thirst for recognition is universal. In gifted people it amounts to a desire for fame or glory.

As a leader you can give recognition and show appreciation in a variety of ways. A sincere 'well done' or 'thank you' can work wonders for a person's morale.

But it is equally important to encourage a climate where each person recognizes the worth or value of the contribution of other members of the team. For it is recognition by our peers – discerning equals or colleagues – that we value even more than the praise of superiors. We are social animals and we thirst for the esteem of others. Without fairly regular payments by others into that deposit account it is hard to maintain the balance of our own self-esteem.

Seize every opportunity, then, to give recognition, even if it is only for effort. We cannot always command results. Perceive the worth of what the other person is doing and show your appreciation. You do not have to be a manager to do that, for true leadership can always be exercised from marginal positions.

CHECKLIST: GIVE RECOGNITION

	Yes	No
Have you yourself ever received some recognition that meant more to you than money?	☐	☐
Why do you think many managers are so reluctant to give recognition?		
1. Because they don't know what is going on.	☐	☐
2. Because they keep the praise for themselves and give the blame to others.	☐	☐
3. Because they lack the skills to give recognition.	☐	☐
4. Because they don't care for people.	☐	☐

List two other reasons:
5. ....
6. ....

Do you know the names of all those who contribute
to the success of your team?   ❏   ❏

How many times did you say 'Thank you' last
week?
1–5 ❏ 6–10 ❏ more than 10 ❏

Does your organization back up words of praise or
recognition with some tangible gift or token?   ❏   ❏

Has the giving of recognition and awards become
rather perfunctory or routine in your organization? ❏   ❏

If you have ticked Yes, what five ways would you
adopt to restore freshness, sincerity and grace?
1. ....
2. ....
3. ....
4. ....
5. ....

KEY POINTS

- Most people value positive recognition. They look for it
  when they know that they have done something
  exceptional – over and above the call of duty.
- Recognition should be given equally, on the basis of merit
  only. It should reward real achievements or contributions
  to the common good.

- Recognition can be given formally or informally. To be of any value it has to be genuine and sincere. Giving it publicly – at a meeting or on a public notice board – reinforces it.
- As a manager, develop an awareness of who is doing what in your organization so that you can pick out real contributors who rarely receive any recognition.
- Knowing people's names is the essential step. To recognize means literally to know again. When you have been recognized, your own personal deed or contribution has been known and valued. You have 'made your name'.
- A gift is a way of giving recognition in a concrete manner. The gift is only a token, like a soldier's medal, but it symbolizes the value of what has been done. It can take many forms, but thought should be invested to ensure that it's fitting.

Any of us will put out more and better ideas if our efforts are fully appreciated.

                                                    Alexander F. Osborn

INDEX